# 18 HOLES WITH BING

# 18 HOLES WITH BING

## GOLF, LIFE, AND LESSONS FROM DAD

## NATHANIEL CROSBY

### AND JOHN STREGE

**DEY ST.**
*AN IMPRINT OF*
WILLIAM MORROW *PUBLISHERS*

HarperCollins books may be purchased for educational, business, or sales pro-motional use. For information please e-mail the Special Markets Department at SPsales@harpercollins.com.

FIRST EDITION

*Designed by Paula Russell Szafranski*
*Frontispiece art by Harry Benson/Getty Images*

Library of Congress Cataloging-in-Publication Data has been applied for.

ISBN 978-0-06-241428-1

16 17 18 19 20   OV/RRD   10 9 8 7 6 5 4 3 2 1

*To my kids, in hopes they will continue the legacy*

*of one-on-one parenting and the pursuit of generational*

*friendships that began with my dad*

# CONTENTS

# FOREWORD

## BY JACK NICKLAUS

One year in the 1960s, I was playing in the Bing Crosby National Pro-Am, and it was my birthday, January 21st. I had several people in my room at the Lodge at Pebble Beach, and we were watching tournament play conclude on the eighteenth hole when the phone rang. My good friend John Swanson was calling to wish me a happy birthday. Then John handed the phone to someone who began singing "Happy Birthday" to me. I could not hear it well above the noise of the crowd in my room and was unable to ascertain who it was. Finally, the man finished the song. I stood there, a bit impatient, and asked somewhat curtly, "With whom am I speaking, please?"

"Oh, Jack," the man on the other end of the line said. "It's Bing Crosby. I just wanted to wish you a happy birthday. I guess my voice must have been hoarse."

I felt about two feet tall. The most famous voice in America was serenading me on my birthday, and I was unable to recognize it. It was possibly my most embarrassing moment in golf—or outside of golf. Fortunately, Bing never held it against me and certainly not against the PGA Tour.

The PGA Tour is indebted to Bing Crosby, whose contributions to professional golf and golfers in the earlier years is immeasurable, including his establishment of the pro-am format that is a staple of every PGA Tour event and the source of much of its charitable contributions. Everyone in the game viewed the Crosby Pro-Am as one of the premier events on the PGA Tour. Major championships were important in those days, but not to the same degree they are now. The Crosby "Clambake" was close to a major in many golfers' eyes, closer certainly than any other tournament on the PGA Tour.

Bing's contributions were not confined to his own tournament, however. He was very kind to me and was always interested in what I was doing and how he might contribute to my own tournament, the Memorial, at Muirfield Village Golf Club in Dublin, Ohio. He came to the tournament, played in the pro-am, and was a great member of our Captains Club, a group of the game's statesmen who select the Memorial's annual Honoree, provide guidance on player invitations and the conduct of our tournament, and frequently meet to discuss topical issues in today's game.

I was always appreciative when Bob Jones would come out to watch me play at Augusta National in the Masters. Similarly, I appreciated it when Bing would come out to watch me play at Pebble Beach. I was fortunate to have won his tournament on three occasions.

Bing, incidentally, was a very good player in his own right, having played in both the U.S. Amateur and the British Amateur. His son Nathaniel was a fine player, too. Nathaniel's U.S. Amateur title at the Olympic Club in 1981 would have been very special for Bing.

One more story: In 1967, the first year that Spyglass Hill was added to the rotation at the Bing Crosby National Pro-Am, Bing proposed a wager. "Jack," he said, "I'm going to bet you five dollars that you can't break par the first time you see Spyglass." I accepted the bet and I shot a two-under-par 70 in a practice round there. I have a nice $5 bill at the Nicklaus Museum, signed by Bing and congratulating me on my 70 at Spyglass.

Bing Crosby was absolutely a great ambassador for our game, and I remember him fondly as a great man and friend as well.

# CHAPTER 1

# AS FAMOUS AS FAMOUS GETS

Bing Crosby, or Dad to me, was the most popular entertainer in the world in his day, a day that lasted the better part of five decades. In the last year of his life, he was still selling out shows in London and New York City. "Just imagine something five times stronger than the popularity of Elvis Presley and the Beatles put together," Tony Bennett, a legend in his own right, said in 1999. Dad's influence spanned generations. According to David Sheff's *The Last Interview*, the Beatles' first hit single, "Please, Please Me," was inspired in part by a line in one of Dad's songs. "I remember the day I wrote it," John Lennon said. "I heard Roy Orbison doing 'Only the Lonely' or something. And I was intrigued by the words to a Bing Crosby song that went, 'Please lend a little ear to my pleas.' The double use of the word 'please.' So it was a combination of Roy Orbison and Bing Crosby."

Billboard called Dad "the most popular radio star of all time." For five years in a row he was the number-one box office draw, and in 1944 he won an Academy Award as best actor for his portrayal of Father O'Malley in *Going My Way*.

He ranks among the best-selling recording artists in history with more than a half billion of his songs and albums in circulation. His recording of "White Christmas" is the best-selling single of all time and remains a holiday standard. Late in his career, he delivered another holiday standard, "Peace on Earth/ Little Drummer Boy," with his unlikely collaborator David Bowie. Generations have been bridged by this voice, which *The Times* of London once wrote had been "heard more often by more people than that of any mortal in history." Between 1927 and 1962 he had 368 charted records. No one else is even close: Frank Sinatra had 209, Elvis Presley 149, and the Beatles 68. In 1960, Dad was presented with a platinum record and honored as "First Citizen of the Record Industry," based on having sold 200 million discs.

But there's more. *Yank*, a weekly military magazine published during World War II, identified him as the individual who had done the most to boost morale during the war, according to U.S. troops polled; President Franklin Roosevelt came in second. In 1947, an *Associated Press* poll identified him as the most admired man alive, ahead of Jackie Robinson and Pope Paul XII.

And then there was golf. Everything Dad accomplished in the entertainment field was a distant second to this game that animated him more than anything else. As my mother so aptly described many years ago, Bing Crosby was a golfer who sang.

"In the battle against par or against your opponent," Dad once told *Golf Digest*, "you can't think about much else, and the result, for me at least, is good therapy. For me, golf has been a kind of passport to relaxation and happiness."

He began the Bing Crosby Pro-Am in 1937; and it still is played today, though under an assumed name, the AT&T Pebble Beach National Pro-Am. The pro-am concept that is a staple of virtually every PGA Tour event today, with proceeds earmarked for charity, was Dad's idea.

Yet with his unsurpassed fame and his exalted standing in the history of both entertainment and golf, he was just Dad to me, albeit with unusually large accommodations. When I was four, he moved the family from Beverly Hills to the San Francisco suburb of Hillsborough. Our home on five acres was somewhere in the vicinity of 20,000 square feet, with 25 rooms. We had a butler, two housekeepers, a gardener, and a governess. The artwork included a variety of western pieces: a Remington, two C.M. Russells, three Herman Hansens; a Jean-Baptiste-Camille Corot, and an Alfred Munnings. Moreover, my mother had a large Faberge collection, accumulated via gifts from my father every year of their twenty-year marriage. None of it meant anything to me until I took an art history class in college and realized the historic significance of much of the family's art collection. When asked on a test where the location of a particular famous rendering was, I answered, "Upstairs at my house."

Adding to the peculiarity of my upbringing was the fact that my father included us in his Christmas specials that aired within a week or two before Christmas each year from 1965 to 1977, the last year of Dad's life. The shows aired on NBC in an era when there were only three networks and a couple local stations from which viewers could choose. As a result, the Christmas shows received Super Bowl–caliber ratings, audiences of fifty million watching us attempt not to embarrass ourselves in skits and songs with Dad and other stars. I was embarrassed regardless, as most kids would be wearing neon leotard outfits with sequins and dancing and singing (with my microphone turned off).

In retrospect, Dad wanted us to have a Hollywood experience, while keeping us at a safe distance from Hollywood, by moving the family from Beverly Hills to Hillsborough. He wanted us to have a normal childhood to the extent it was possible with a famous father.

Dad ensured we all had ample time alone with him, which for me included sharing season tickets to the San Francisco 49ers, attending the Pittsburgh Pirates' games when they played the Giants at Candlestick Park, playing golf together at the Burlingame Country Club several times a week, and competing in junior golf tournaments, where he would watch me through binoculars from several fairways away to avoid drawing attention to himself.

I was just turning sixteen when Dad died in October 1977, leaving me with an emotional void. My mother soon left on a theater tour, my brother and sister were gone, and I was left largely to fend for myself in the large Hillsborough mansion. Dad's death at seventy-four was at the time considered a reasonably long life, yet it still came as a shock and was not easy for any of us. There isn't a roadmap for fatherless teens or, as I told my mother years later, for widows at forty-three.

Golf, meanwhile, continued to be the focal point of my youth, and the experiences I had had at the Bing Crosby National Pro-Am, handing out scorecards and pencils to the likes of Arnold Palmer, Jack Nicklaus, Lee Trevino, and others, motivated me to work hard on my golf with the intention of playing the PGA Tour one day.

I fell short on that front, but I did win one very important tournament, the U.S. Amateur Championship in 1981, less than four years after my father's death. I had been inspired by a cause greater than myself; I wanted to win to honor my father's memory.

The victory landed me on the cover of *Golf World* magazine and was national news. *Golf Digest, Sports Illustrated, Golf* magazine, *The New York Times*, even *People* magazine all had stories, principally because of the country's enduring affection for my father, the entertainment legend. But there was something else at play, too: his love of golf and his history with the game.

Dad was a strong enough golfer to have played in the U.S. Amateur himself, in 1940, at Winged Foot Golf Club in Mamaroneck, New York, outside New York City. He also played in the British Amateur one year and countless other lesser amateur competitions. I had found a medal my father had received for participating in one of them, and I wore it on a chain around my neck throughout the 1981 Amateur, rubbing it for good luck in stressful situations. My mother, meanwhile, wore Dad's old sport coat and hat during the final match.

Dad was a remarkably humble man, even with his lengthy record of achievement, and he expected the same of his kids.

A reporter asked me what my father might have said had he been there to witness my victory. "Don't let it go to your head, son," I replied. Privately, I'm sure he would have had another reaction, one closer to that of his old road partner and golf foil, Bob Hope, seventy-eight at the time, and who was watching the telecast in the grillroom of a Minnesota golf club. When I holed the winning putt, I was told by an assistant professional at the club that Bob had cried. Hope's emotional reaction was a testament to his long and adoring friendship with my father and his understanding of what it would have meant to Dad had he been there.

He also understood what golf meant to my father.

My father, even during the Depression years that had eliminated disposable income for most, was a major contributor to a golf boom as a result of the attention he helped bring to the game during the war and after. He and Bob Hope played in countless exhibition golf matches with Ben Hogan, Jimmy Demaret, and others to raise funds for the war effort. After the war, he put golf on a mainstream stage for the first time when he resumed the Bing Crosby National Pro-Am, moved it to Pebble Beach, and eventually put it on television.

Former USGA Executive Director David Fay noted Dad's contributions to golf in an interview with *Sports Illustrated* in 2008: "You can't quantify what Bing Crosby did for golf," Fay said. "But you can't overstate it, either."

This book is my tribute to him.

# CHAPTER 2

# GRASS ROOTS

Dad's game of choice originally was baseball, which he began playing in elementary school. He was an infielder at Gonzaga Prep in Spokane, Washington, and later played a season at Gonzaga University. He also played football and basketball in a youth program called the Junior Yard Association. But his best sport in his youth was swimming.

His introduction to golf came through the caddy ranks at Downriver Golf Course in Spokane, where he earned fifty cents per bag per round. When he was done playing baseball and had started to dabble in music, he returned to Downriver with bandmate Al Rinker and they began playing golf together, establishing the foundation of what would become an obsession.

When the two of them took their musical talents and ambitions to Los Angeles late in 1925, his passion for the game began to take root. They often played at Griffith Park Golf Course, which in those days was an unkempt municipal course that featured sand greens that were a detriment to the enjoyment of the game. So were its green fees for a pair of neophyte entertainers attempting to scratch out a living. So when they discovered that an aspiring musician, who frequently hung around backstage at the Metropolitan Theater at which Dad and Rinker were performing, also was a golf pro at the private Bel-Air Country Club above Beverly Hills, they concocted a plan—or "Machiavellian gimmick," as my father called it. They feigned an interest in the pro's songwriting, and in turn he allowed them access to the Bel-Air course at dawn, so long as they completed their rounds by nine, when the members tended to tee off.

Their Machiavellian gimmick worked better than they had anticipated. One morning, they arrived late and were on the green at the par-three tenth hole when a wealthy member arrived at the tee. Unable to hide, they stepped to the side of the green to allow him to play through. The man hooked his tee shot and the ball came bounding toward my father, who instinctively kicked it back toward the green. It turned out that Dad's "foot wedge" was his best shot of the day; the ball rolled toward the pin and eventually into the hole. When the member reached the green he asked them if they'd seen his ball. It was suggested that he look in the hole. His ensuing euphoria was sufficient that he ignored the fact that his eyewitnesses were trespassing; ultimately the scofflaws were rewarded with guest-privilege cards good for two months of free golf on one of Los Angeles's finest courses.

But the game gives and it takes, to which every golfer can attest. Many years later, Dad had a house built adjacent to the fourteenth fairway of the North Course at Los Angeles Country Club, one of the finest courses in the country and, incidentally, scheduled to host the U.S. Open for the first time in 2023. Yet he was rebuffed in his effort to join the club when the membership invoked its longstanding policy of keeping entertainers out. It was Los Angeles Country Club that had denied a membership request from Groucho Marx, eliciting his famous rejoinder, "Why would I want to belong to a club that would have me as a member?" Victor Mature also was rejected for membership on the grounds that he was an actor. "Hell, I'm no actor," he said, "and I've got twenty-eight pictures and a scrapbook of reviews to prove it." As for Dad, the logical assumption is that he thought he could force the issue with his house adjacent to the course. If so, it didn't work. It was the one thorn in his side that he could never remove.

Otherwise, he had virtual carte blanche to whatever courses he wished to play. He had memberships at seventy-five country clubs, according to my mother, Kathryn Crosby, "most of them to which we paid dues," she said (feigning indignation). In fact, many were honorary memberships, but among those that weren't was a collection of some of the finest clubs in the country, including the Cypress Point Club in Pebble Beach, San Francisco Golf Club, and Seminole Golf Club in Juno Beach, Florida.

MY FATHER WAS A STRONG PLAYER, WHO WON HIS CLUB championship at Lakeside five times between 1936 and 1943.

His swing was what one might expect from a crooner—smooth, with perfect tempo. *The New Yorker* writer Herbert Warren Wind described his swing as "legato."

Dad was a good enough player to have qualified to play in the U.S. Amateur in 1940. His friend, the talented tour pro and former Masters champion Jackie Burke Jr., and my godfather, noted that "his short game was as good as any pro I've ever known. He had an unbelievable touch with his hands, tremendous timing, because he always had that in music, too."

The U.S. Amateur in 1940 was played at Winged Foot Golf Club near New York City. Predictably, given Dad's standing in the entertainment world at the time, bedlam ensued—huge, unruly galleries of which even Joe Louis, the heavyweight champion of the world at the time, was a part. My father apparently was a rock star before there were rock stars. "His fans, mostly women, swarmed all over the course, straining to catch sight of him," Robert Sommers wrote in *Golf Journal.* "The crowd grew so large and so unruly that the club called in New York State troopers to protect him and his partners." *Time* magazine wrote, "Twittering around the first tee of suburban New York's Winged Foot Golf Club last week were flocks of women in high-heeled pumps . . . The golfer they had gone to see was crooner Bing Crosby."

Bamboo poles ordinarily used for sweeping dew from the greens in the mornings were used to keep the throngs at bay, though on the last hole of the second stroke-play round they broke through and swarmed him. State troopers needed fifteen minutes to clear the fairway so he and his playing partners could complete their rounds.

Dad shot 83–77 in the medal rounds and did not advance to the match play part of the championship. One of his playing partners for those two rounds was Patrick Mucci, who wrote, "He could have qualified [for match play], but due to the huge galleries and their behavior he missed."

In 1950, Dad made a second attempt at competing at the elite amateur level by entering the British Amateur on the Old Course at St. Andrews, where the scenario he had encountered at Winged Foot a decade earlier repeated itself but on a larger scale. He entered the tournament under his given name, Harry L. Crosby, but the ruse did not work. "Two-thousand giggling lassies tore the silent Scottish Sabbath to shrieking shreds," the *Associated Press* wrote of his first day in town. "That's how the Scots learned Bing Crosby had arrived."

The next day was worse. "Dozens of buses and number-less private cars converged on that speck of eastern Fife, and approximately twenty thousand fans were soon packed along the borders of the course," Herbert Warren Wind wrote in *The New Yorker*. Dad opened with three birdies to take a three-up lead on local carpenter J.K. Wilson, but on the fourth hole he played to the wrong green. He also began shanking shots. He eventually lost the match, three and two. "I have an idea that he did not want to create such a crowd scene again—he hadn't expected anything like it—and intentionally let a few holes slip away as the round wore on," Wind wrote.

The greatest shot of my father's life was an expensive one. It came on the sixteenth hole at Cypress Point Club in Pebble Beach, "the greatest par three in the world," he called it. Even today few would argue otherwise. Dad described it as a

220-yard carry over an inlet of ocean—"mollusk country," he called it—to the front of the green, with the wind whipping and the waves crashing.

On this particular day in 1948, the hole was playing 222 yards with the wind blowing. He made the second hole-in-one ever there. "I was shooting into the sun, so I just stood up and smacked one blind," he told the press. "The caddy said it looked pretty close, but I didn't think it was in the hole." It was one of thirteen aces he made in his life, and he was going to pay for it.

"I was playing with a group that included Stuart Haldorn, an old chap, a member who'd only go about three holes, then drive up to the clubhouse and watch the rest of the way with field glasses," Dad said. "Well, I hit one through the mist with my driver. Haldorn saw the ball going into the hole, and he started calling members on the phone. By the time I got to the clubhouse, there was quite a quorum present. The bar was opened and the drinks, of course, were on me. The tab went about $700, but it was well worth it, considering the magnitude of the exploit."

Dad's happiest days were any that were spent on a golf course. In 1958, Joan Flynn Dreyspool wrote an excellent article on my father for *Sports Illustrated*. Dad was explaining to her the importance of golf in his life. "Golf has been very good to me, and I'm grateful," he said. "Being a fair player, it has been possible for me, anywhere I go all over the world, to establish associations and friendships and to entertain myself in a healthy, relaxing exercise. As a fellow who travels quite a great deal, that has always seemed important to me. I can always find a golf game, whether it's in Pocatello or Popocatepetl. I compliment myself, also, that, although approaching my mid-fifties, I can still make a decent showing in competitive golf. I don't know any other sport where this could be possible. But I suppose I'm most grateful to golf because, through the years, it has provided such a wonderful relief from tensions, from the problems of show business. I've found that the golf links is not a place for brooding or soul-wrestling. You leave all that on the first tee, and you feel a lot better when you come in."

The great *Los Angeles Times* columnist Jim Murray, a newspaper legend, was one of my father's favorites, to the extent that when he was traveling he had his secretary mail him Murray's columns. It was impossible not to like Murray, personally or professionally, but my father's affection for him likely also was based on the fact that Murray understood him. "No one loved golf like Bing Crosby," Murray wrote. "I never had a conversation with him in the twenty-five years I knew him that didn't begin or end with golf. 'How you hittin' them?' was his standard opening line."

Throughout his adult life, my father was determined to play golf whenever he could and wherever he was. On a long layover in Chicago one March day, the weather cold and wet, Dad was in the lobby of the Conrad Hilton Hotel; he went to a pay phone to call an old friend, Charley Penna, the pro at Beverly Country Club there, to see if he'd be interested in playing a quick round.

"Charley? This is Bing Crosby," Dad said.

"Cut out the kidding," Penna replied. "Who is this?"

"It's Crosby."

"If you're Crosby, let's hear you sing."

So there in the lobby of the Conrad Hilton Hotel, Dad began singing, providing those within earshot a short impromptu concert from one of the most famous voices in the world. Penna quickly concluded it indeed was Crosby, apologized, and agreed to a game. They played eleven holes before a downpour sent them scrambling back to the clubhouse. A few hours later, Dad was on a plane to London.

Initially, his radio shows were broadcast live, requiring him to do one show for the East Coast audience, then a second show for the West Coast audience. But in the wake of World War II, American engineers in Germany learned that the Nazis had discovered how to record on magnetic tape, a leap in recording technology, and were using it to spread their propaganda. Dad learned about it, and it piqued his interest. He invested $50,000 in Ampex, the company that developed the technology, with the intention of taping the shows to free up more time for golf.

In 1947, when NBC insisted his show continue to air live, he took his recording device and went to ABC. "There was considerable to-do when I broke away from the customary practice in big radio shows to [record] my shows . . . as long as two months in advance of the Wednesday nights when you hear them," he wrote. "Golf had plenty to do with my decision to present [recorded] shows. The demands of the radio deadlines and the inconvenience of being at a studio for rehearsals and shows week after week at the same time were interfering with my golf. My golf is too important to my business performances to be interfered with."

Thus, Dad became "a grandfather to the computer hard drive and an angel investor in one of the firms that created Silicon Valley," Paul Ford wrote in *The New Yorker*.

His first recorded show for ABC allowed him the opportunity to play in the Totem Pole Tournament at the Jasper Park Lodge Golf Course in Canada, a course with which he had acquainted himself the summer before when he was filming *The Emperor Waltz* in the area. The reviews of the recorded shows, incidentally, were exceptional, including this one from the *Hollywood Citizen News*: "The new method of recording *The Bing Crosby Show* is far superior to that used previously. The program came over sharper, clearer, and truer than last year. The singer had a more enjoyable program for another reason—he didn't give the impression that he was bored and wishing he were somewhere other than before the microphone."

Dad, incidentally, won the Totem Pole Tournament. In the thirty-six-hole final, he and his opponent Gordon Verley were tied at the last hole. The *Jasper Tourist News* reported:

Verley was only about a foot from the pin on his third while Bing's second lay beyond the green, at least 30 feet astray of the mark. From this position Bing couldn't see the pin. He was under the shade of a massive Douglas fir. To make matters more despairing a youngster maintained constant squirming just behind him. The Hollywood ace took his stance then broke it with a good-humored offer to change places with the lad. This little act cut the tension

for the big gallery, and Bing followed up by almost non-
chalantly chipping the ball into the cup.

In my mother's book *My Life with Bing*, she recalled a European trip they took together in 1960, one that included attending the Olympic Games in Rome, an audience with Pope
John XXIII at the Vatican, and a golf tournament, the Mittersill
Invitational, in Austria. Dad won both low net and low gross in
the tournament. "I'm sure that the Pope would have been sorry
to hear it," Mom wrote, "but [the tournament] was the height
of the tour for Bing."

In the late 1960s, Dad was offered the lead in the television show *Columbo*. "He was the first choice, and they offered
it to him, but he had a golf tournament," Peter Falk said in
2003. Falk had gotten the role instead and became, as one his-
torian described him, "everyone's favorite rumpled television
detective."

"I guess I'm making it tough on my agent," Dad told
*TV Guide*. "I seem to be arranging my work around other
activities."

Or activity. My mother enjoys telling a story about how
much golf meant to my father. My sister, Mary Frances, was
an aspiring actress and later an accomplished one, whose character, Kristen Shepard, in the hit television series *Dallas* was
the answer to the most pressing question in television in the
summer of 1980: Who shot J.R.? Four years earlier, she and my
mother were in Texas performing together in a play called *The
Latest Mrs. Adams*.

One Saturday, Dad called her and breathlessly said, "This is the happiest day of my life. Nathaniel has just won the men's club championship at Burlingame County club."

Mom was understandably offended. "That was Bing's happiest day," she said. "Not the songs or the films or any of his show business successes. Not our wedding. Not the birth of his little girl. The fact that his teenage son had become the men's champion at the Burlingame Country Club."

She was offended, but probably not surprised.

Dad's first wife, Dixie Lee, had died of cancer in 1952. In 1957, he married Kathryn Grant, my mother. Between marriages, he was linked romantically to a number of interesting women, including Ingrid Bergman, with whom he starred in *The Bells of St. Mary's*; Inger Stevens, whom he met doing the film *Man on Fire*; and Grace Kelly, his co-star in *The Country Girl* and *High Anxiety*. Many years after his death, Mom did an autobiographical stage show loosely based on her book in which she featured large photos of Dad's love interests. She concluded by saying simply, "I won."

It was a hollow victory of sorts, as she learned in the early years of her marriage, when she realized she had to share his affections with golf. Each day after playing a round of golf, Dad would come home and tell her about his round. After about eight years of marriage, she finally asked him, "Have you ever gotten better?"

"Probably not," he replied. "It's probably as good as I'm ever going to get."

It did not deter him from trying, virtually every day his

schedule permitted. Mom indeed had won out over Grace Kelly and others, but ultimately she lost to golf, Dad's true paramour. She was a bona fide golf widow.

And on one special occasion a punch line. There was a thirty-year age difference between them. This wasn't unusual in Hollywood, or, for that matter, Texas, where Mom was from. On their wedding day in Las Vegas, Dad, in front of his new bride and standing by his plane waiting to depart, was fielding questions from about forty reporters who had made the dash from Los Angeles through the night after learning of their early-morning wedding.

"Mr. Crosby, in ten years you will be sixty-two years old and Kathryn will only be thirty-two years old. What will you do then?"

Dad, visibly uncomfortable and even embarrassed by the question, paused for the longest time.

"Well," he finally said, "I guess I'll have to trade her in on a new model."

# CHAPTER 3

# THE JAZZ SINGER

Bing Crosby might have become a lawyer. Ponder the historical ramifications had that happened—for golf certainly—but for the greater world of music, particularly jazz. Dad isn't often identified with jazz, but he was a pioneer in the craft of jazz singing. "Like so many aspects of jazz and pop singing, the movement began with Bing Crosby, who may have influenced even more black singers in the 1930s and 1940s than he did white Italian- and Irish-Americans," Wall Street Journal jazz critic Will Friedwald wrote in his book *Jazz Singing*. Friedwald noted that my father and Louis Armstrong "learned so much from each other that no one could tell which mannerism had begun with which man, and as Mezz Mezzrow tells us, their records mutually flooded the jukeboxes of Harlem, and, presumably, of other black communities across the country."

But he set out to become a lawyer. He was in law school at Gonzaga University in Spokane, Washington, but, in the meantime, was a semiprofessional musician, who at twenty-two had formed a duo with a seventeen-year-old, Al Rinker, who was a saxophone player with a modest singing voice.

Golf had not yet brought Dad under its addictive spell, though Rinker and he had begun playing golf together at Downriver Golf Course in Spokane. Rinker, a poor student, had no future of which to speak, so he considered whatever options he had and chose to persuade Dad to continue to pursue music. Honing their act, notwithstanding Rinker's vocal limitations, they began to harmonize, eventually creating a sound that had potential.

The duo had regular gigs and was earning money, so Dad chose to quit law school and along with Rinker take their show on the road. Rinker suggested heading to Los Angeles, where his sister Mildred Bailey was singing, hoping that she could help land them some gigs. They bought a jalopy with their meager savings, packed it with a couple of suitcases, a drum set, and a set of golf clubs, and . . . the car wouldn't start. Dad borrowed a screwdriver, fixed the issue, and they were off to Los Angeles, at thirty miles an hour. Three weeks later, they reached Los Angeles. Along the way, they had rehearsed and harmonized, time well spent for the coming weeks and months.

They went straight to the home of Mildred Bailey. She began making cocktails and listening to them sing. "You guys are great and will have no problems getting work in this town," she said.

Mildred acted as their agent, helping them find gigs, a favor Dad would later return by introducing her to renowned bandleader Paul Whiteman. Mildred went on to become a jazz legend known as the "Queen of Swing."

Whiteman's business manager, meanwhile, had seen Dad and Rinker perform at the Metropolitan Theater in Los Angeles and came away impressed enough to introduce them to Whiteman. Dad recalled being ushered into Whiteman's dressing room and encountering him reclined on his bed with champagne and caviar, "looking like a Buddha." This, Dad deduced, was what success must look like.

They performed a few songs for Whiteman, who already had been convinced to hire them based on a report he had heard from his violinist and arranger Matty Malneck. He had told Whiteman that it was akin to hearing "a great jazz player for the first time." Whiteman hired them at $150 a week.

They began their association with Whiteman in Chicago and were a hit. Whiteman took Dad to the Sunset Theater there where they saw Louis Armstrong and other talented musicians who were taking jazz mainstream. Dad became a devotee who learned from them as he was developing his own style. Decades later, when Dad was asked who influenced him the most he replied, "I am proud to acknowledge my debt to Reverend Satchelmouth. He is the beginning and the end of music in America. Long may he reign."

Whiteman was a superstar long before the word was ever coined. Whiteman had had the luxury and the budget to recruit the best jazz performers in the country, many of whom Dad befriended and with whom he worked, including Bix

Beiderbecke, Eddie Lang, Joe Venuti, Frank Trumbauer, Jack Teagarden, and others.

These were Dad's friends and teammates early in his career, which centered on scat music and jazz. They played a significant role in the foundation of jazz, as we know it today.

My father and Bix became close friends and drinking buddies, even sharing a room at the Belvedere Hotel in New York City. They frequented a speakeasy there, where Bix and other accomplished musicians exchanged ideas while Dad listened attentively, hoping to learn from them. Bix eventually was considered one of the most influential jazz soloists of the early twentieth century. He had four number-one hits under Whiteman's recording label, all with Dad as the lead vocalist. Alas, Bix had health issues related to excessive drinking and was only twenty-eight when he died.

Dad and Rinker were less successful in New York than they had been in Chicago, at least until Malneck stepped up again and introduced them to Harry Barris, a high-energy piano player he thought might enliven their act. This was the start of the famed Rhythm Boys, the group that launched Dad to stardom.

Barris was an accomplished songwriter and the Rhythm Boys opened with one of his new songs called "Mississippi Mud." The song was scat music at its finest. More hits followed, as did success.

Dad's interest in golf, meanwhile, was growing into a genuine addiction during the Rhythm Boys' vaudeville tour with Whiteman. At one point they were scheduled to perform forty weeks in a row and the exhaustive schedule began to take its toll. "There were trains we missed and bags that didn't arrive," Dad said. "We didn't let such mishaps interfere with our golf. We got a game in every morning if we could find a course."

Eventually Whiteman became disillusioned with Dad and Rinker. "Whiteman criticized the duo for always chasing girls and wanting to play golf," one account said. In the midst of the filming of *The King of Jazz*, Dad had a court appointment on a drunk-driving charge and he showed up in knickers and golf shoes. "Don't you know there's a prohibition law?" the judge asked. "Yeah," Dad reportedly said, "but nobody pays much attention to it." The judge took offense at what he perceived to be a lack of respect both in his attire and his demeanor and sentenced him to thirty days in jail, with a daytime work furlough.

Some time after the movie was completed, the Rhythm Boys were en route to play shows in Seattle and Portland when Dad and Whiteman began arguing over a bootlegger's bill. "A bootlegger who followed the band selling some day-old 'pop skull' claimed that I owed him for a bottle of his sauce," Dad said. "I owed him nothing and I said so, but Pops Whiteman paid him anyhow and took it out of my salary."

It spelled the end of their relationship. "You don't seem to be too serious," Whiteman said. "You're just having a good time living off of the fat of the land and getting arrested and costing me money. When we get to Seattle we will part as friends and that will be the end of it."

By then, Dad's star was ascending and his future was bright. His experiences with Whiteman had been invaluable, including his growing friendship with Louis Armstrong, who later became one of the most important figures in jazz history and a fixture in my father's career. When Dad was in New York, he used to walk from midtown Manhattan to the Cotton Club in Harlem to listen to Armstrong and other jazz notables such as Cab Calloway, Duke Ellington, and Fletcher Henderson, all of whom had an influence on him. Those performances by jazz legends helped start his transition from scat music into his style of combining crooning and jazz variations.

Armstrong and Dad formed a lifelong friendship and working relationship. Armstrong was a regular guest on Dad's radio show, and eventually Dad cast him in a supporting role in the film *Pennies From Heaven*. He gave him equal billing with white actors in the film, a Hollywood first. "I really think Bing was right at home when he could have his pipe and Pops [Louis Armstrong]," the great jazz pianist Count Basie said. "I think that was really his life, anything he and Louis could do. They fit so good. Bing and Pops were something together." He frequently invited Armstrong to perform on his television shows and additional films, including *Here Comes the Groom* and *High Society*.

When Armstrong died in 1971, Dad was among his pallbearers.

My father's legacy on the jazz front often has been overlooked, though not by everyone. "The young Crosby was one of the hottest jazzmen around, the first singer to popularize a gentle, conversational style speckled with held notes like groans, a pioneer who traded innovations with good friend Louis Armstrong and may well have been the single most influential American musician of the twentieth century," Peter Goodman wrote in *Newsday*.

Dad also paid homage to Whiteman. "When I was young and more hot headed," he said, "I used to think that he should line my pockets full of more gold. But I confess he owes me nothing. It's the other way around.

As for his golf, well, music is dependent on rhythm and tempo. So is golf. And Dad had both. "He played the game," the great *Los Angeles Times* columnist Jim Murray wrote, "with the same rhythm and style as he sang 'Melancholy Baby.' "

Or, as *Saturday Night Live* comedian Dennis Miller put it, "Hip? I think he embodied the word. The Mick Jagger of 1926. Mr. Cool. The guy did it all."

# CHAPTER 4

# THE WAR YEARS

On December 7, 1941, Bob Hope and my father were together at the home of President Roosevelt's son Elliott in Colorado Springs, Colorado. "When the news came from Pearl Harbor, we decided to join the Navy," Hope wrote in his book *Bob Hope's Confessions of a Hooker*. "Elliott got on the phone with his father in the White House and with Frank Knox, the Secretary of the Navy. Knox wanted to give us commissions in the Navy, but FDR said, 'No, we don't want 'em in the Navy. We want 'em to do just what they're doing—entertaining the troops.' "

I can't say whether they truly intended to join the Navy, but indisputably they took their ensuing responsibilities seriously, and their contributions to the war effort were notable. Dad, as was Hope, was selfless in contributing however he could, without regard to inconvenience, whatever the cause, wherever it took him. In 1944, it took him to the European theater as the headliner on a USO tour. He traveled via the French ocean liner, *Ile De France*, that had been converted to transport as many as 1,500 paratroopers from New York to Scotland. Quarters were tight; Dad said they were packed together the way "brides spoon."

Dad recalled one trooper in particular. "A big tough Irish paratrooper with a chin like a landing barge. Stationed himself outside my door and waylaid me," Dad said. "When I came out, he said, 'Sing me a song.'

'I don't have accompaniment here,' Dad replied. 'I ought to have at least a guitar.'

'Oh, yeah? You don't want to sing me a song, then the hell with you. Come on, sing me a song.' "

Dad was doing as many as five one-hour shows a day aboard the ship and attempted unsuccessfully to convince the trooper to see one of them. Finally, on the day they were supposed to arrive in Scotland, he was cornered again and succumbed. He sang "Sweet Leilani."

"Not bad," the trooper said before returning to his card game.

"Evidently, he'd been trained not to give up until he'd obtained his objective," Dad said later. "I'll say this for him, he had Situation Crosby under control."

Dad was able to make light of it, but the trip was hard work. He was seasick much of the time, but still performed the shows so that all the troops had an opportunity to see him. "Crosby worked harder than anybody; he endeared himself to everyone aboard the ship," Don Stanford, author of a book on the *Ile De France*, wrote.

When Dad arrived in London, the Offices of Strategic Services thought it might be a good idea for him to broadcast directly to the German people. Thus the moniker "Der Bingle" was conceived. Dad sang relentlessly and delivered messages explaining to anyone listening that Americans live in a free country, without a Gestapo to fear, and that all peoples were welcome. Der Bingle was Dad's version of Tokyo Rose, who delivered Japanese propaganda to American servicemen in the South Pacific.

DAD WENT FROM SCOTLAND TO CHERBOURG ON THE NORTH coast of France about six weeks after D-Day. They followed the troops down the peninsula, on into Paris, and finally to Metz and Nancy, where there was still fighting. They performed three shows a day for troops and visited the wounded in field hospitals between shows. "The look on the faces of those we entertained was better than any money from Paramount [Studios]," he wrote.

"At one point in the tour we were working out of General [Omar] Bradley's headquarters. In addition to performing for the GI audiences in the various encampments it was considered important to entertain the smaller groups in the outposts. So at the start of the day I would get in a jeep and go around to the outposts, putting on little shows and talking to the boys."

Dad's friend Fred Astaire had issued him two warnings: Don't sleep near a bridge, and when in a jeep, watch the telephone wires. "When you can't see them anymore, you're in trouble," he said.

On the first night Dad was thinking about how nice the accommodations were, considering they were on the front lines. Then he looked out the window and spotted a bridge. He came outside and immediately told the soldier that he would prefer to sleep in a shack that he had spotted up on a hill. Dad had his way and sure enough the bridge and his original accommodation were blown up that night.

Later during that campaign, while still working out of General Bradley's headquarters, Dad and a lieutenant were out in a jeep. The officer was armed to the hilt. They were going down a dusty road when Dad noticed that the telephone wires had stopped. Dad suggested that they turn around and the officer agreed, saying that they might be in "No Man's Land." That night Dad was invited to General Bradley's headquarters and the general asked him where he'd been that day.

"We made it to the town of St. Mere Eglise," Dad said.

"St. Mere Eglise?" Bradley said incredulously. "We haven't taken St. Mere Eglise yet!"

"Well, we had it for a while this morning," Dad said in his best deadpan. "I can't believe that you've lost it already."

Shortly before Dad's tour was over he was visiting General Eisenhower's headquarters in Versailles. A note awaited him, stating that a Colonel Galt wanted to see him. Dad told a friend about the note, and the friend informed him that Colonel Galt was Eisenhower's aide and that it probably meant that the general wanted to see him.

The friend then told Dad to request a car should Eisenhower ask whether he could do anything for him. Sure enough, when Dad met with Eisenhower, the general asked him whether he needed anything and Dad responded as he had been instructed.

Cars were difficult to get, yet Eisenhower loaned him his own, complete with the general's five stars emblazoned on the side. Ike said Dad could use as it as long he wanted. Dad and the car made it to most of the Parisian nightclubs over the following four nights and, not surprisingly, given the five stars, he never had an issue with parking.

When Dad finally returned the car, he asked the general if there was anything that he might do for him in return. Eisenhower replied that he was unable to get hominy grits in Europe, and that no one even knew what they were. When Dad returned to New York, he did a radio show and explained the general's plight. No doubt thousands of southern ladies who fancied their grits to be the best shipped their recipes directly to the general's headquarters, until Ike had had enough. He phoned my dad and told him to get back on the radio and "call off the grits."

DAD'S ITINERARY ON THE TOUR WAS EXHAUSTING: SEPTEM-ber 9th, a concert at the American Red Cross club; September 10th, a concert for the personnel of the Supreme Headquarters Allied Expeditionary Force; September 11th, a concert for servicemen at the Ninth Air Force headquarters and another for the Ninth Air Force Service Command; September 12th, a concert with Dinah Shore for General Patton's Third Army. It went on like this for another few weeks.

Eventually, he returned to London, which was under siege from the German's new V-2, the first long-range, guided bal-

listic missile. Dad was involved in entertaining civilians, giving several concerts in and around London. When the sirens
sounded, virtually every evening, Dad joined the civilians in
heading to the Underground, London's subway system, which
was doubling as a shelter. Dad gave makeshift concerts and led
his audience in a chorus of a popular song refrain then:

> *Hitler has one big ball,*
> *Göring has two but very small,*
> *Himmler is very sim'lar*
> *But Goebbels has no balls at all.*

Dad loved the song "White Christmas," but he confessed
that it pained him to sing it to the troops under such circum-
stances. "It was always a kind of a wrench for me to sing the
song," he said. "I loved it of course, but at the camps and in
the field hospitals, places where spirits weren't too high anyway, they'd ask for the song—they'd demand it—and half the
audience would be in tears. It was a rather lugubrious atmo-
sphere that it created, which you can understand, because
of its connotation of home and Christmas, and here we were
thousands of miles from either one. It was a rather sorrowing
experience to have to sing it for these men and women when it
made them feel sad. But I guess in retrospect that it was a glad
kind of sadness."

My father genuinely considered it the least he could do on
behalf of those sacrificing so much more. "Nothing I've ever
done stands out like my trip overseas to entertain the troops in
England and France during the last war," he wrote. "If I never

do anything else, I'll always take satisfaction in knowing that I helped some of our soldiers relax for a few moments when they needed amusement and entertainment."

I especially appreciate what Chaplain James Good Brown wrote in his book *The Mighty Men of the 381st: Heroes All*: "I had quite a conversation with Crosby before the show began as he was waiting for the men to get the stage arranged in the proper manner. He thoroughly enjoys going around to the war camps and bases. To him, it is both fun and a patriotic duty. He feels that it is the way he can do his part in this war. Neither did I hesitate to tell him I thought he was doing as much good for the men as the chaplain. To this he remarked, 'Not quite as much good as you chaplains are doing.' "

A radio columnist, Ralph K. Bellamy, gave this brief synopsis of his trip: "During Bing's four weeks at the front in France, he performed under any and all conditions, during bombings and artillery barrages, and in any kind of weather. He averaged about three shows a day, each lasting about an hour and a half; 'The Groaner' finished off every day's work with a visit to the hospitals."

The *United Press* assembled these statistics from the trip: He spent six and a half weeks overseas, sang 2,250 songs, and played no golf.

There was one brief side trip worth mentioning. Dad traveled to the village of Warton in Lancashire, England, to entertain troops. He was told of three children who had survived the crash of an American B-24 Liberator into their school nearby; the accident had killed thirty-eight of their schoolmates. He went to the hospital to visit the young survivors, one of them a five-year-old girl, Ruby. A story in *Flypast* magazine entitled "The Day Freckleton Wept" recounted his visit:

> Ruby said he sat on her bed and held the tips of her fingers that were sticking out of the bandages. He asked if she would like him to sing him something for her. All she could think of were two songs that her mum always sang: "White Christmas" and "Don't Fence Me In." But Ruby said that the sight of the three tots lying there proved too much for him and Bing could not sing a note. He finally got up and went out into the hall to compose himself. Then he came back and stood in the doorway and sang the two songs which had been requested.

# CHAPTER 5

# A BRITISH BOND

It is not widely known outside of St. Andrews, Scotland, but a Crosby golf tournament is still played there today. The Bing Crosby Trophy is an annual competition that Dad started in 1972 on the Old Course at St. Andrews for St. Andrews Golf Club members sixty years of age and older. Dad loved playing golf in Great Britain and Ireland, home of many of the finest courses in the world. The people there loved him in kind, as an entertainer, of course, but also as one who used his celebrity and talent to help the war effort. The Rusacks Hotel that overlooks the eighteenth hole of the Old Course even features a Bing Crosby Room. The Bing Crosby Trophy was his paean to the home of golf.

Dad first traveled to St. Andrews in 1950 to play in the British Amateur. He lost in the first round to a local carpenter, J.K. Wilson, with whom he formed an enduring friendship that started with this single round. His bond with the British people only deepened from that day. "From the moment the crooner ambled onto the sacred acres of St. Andrews' old course he owned the huge crowd of 4,000 which broke all records for the first day of this 65-year-old tournament," an *Associated Press* report said. Dad, after the press had criticized him for not playing a practice round on the Old Course, started with three birdies. Then he developed a case of the shanks and eventually lost, two-up.

The following year, he was elected to the prestigious Royal and Ancient Golf Club of St. Andrews. He had been nominated by the first American captain of the Royal and Ancient, Francis Ouimet, who at nineteen had launched the American golf revolution by beating Englishmen Harry Vardon and Ted Ray to win the U.S. Open in 1913.

Over time, my father evolved into a certifiable anglophile, and he once wrote that generally he preferred playing British courses to U.S. courses. He returned to Britain and Ireland often, always scheduling golf around his business. Or business around his golf. I found in his files these notes, handwritten on five pages of Stafford Hotel stationery, from a business trip he made to London by way of Scotland in August, 1971 (note that business is not mentioned):

> Aug 4th S.F. to Prestwick via N.Y.—arr 9:30 a.m. 5th, 1 hour drive up to Glen Eagles. Found courses, Kings and Queens, in grand shape—Sherrill, Van Gerbig, Coleman, Hank Ketcham. Good game. Drove to Turnberry (2-1/2 hrs). Marvelous links type course on the sea. Had a 76. Big hotel there which looked quite good. Also drove to St. Andrews for game with Ketcham and Wilson. Big mob scene

around clubhouse. Had to go by Wilson's club to meet his pals—second mob scene. Had nice lunch at R&A. Lady in charge gave us all a big shot of R&A #1 scotch especially bottled for them. Smooth! On 12th drove down to Muirfield (about 1-1/2 hours) for 27 holes. This is the greatest! Shot that back nine in par. Birdied both 3 pars. Lovely old clubhouse. Secretary gave us a great lunch and extended every amenity. Small charming hotel right next to clubhouse (Grey Walls). No par on the card for each hole, because it never plays the same. Our still day a 410 yd hole would be a 4 par. When wind is up its a 5. Constantly changing. Caught 7:00 plane for London. Shopped around London next day and golfed at Sunningdale Sat and Sunday. Dalton, Ian Cooper, Andrew McCain. Monday went up to Brancaster to see P Ward-Thomas. Norfolk lovely country. Bright sunny day. Played with Tom Harvey, Pat, Bobbie Selway. Good players. Great links course right on the sea [Royal West Norfolk Golf Club], windy along through the dunes! Very austere clubhouse. On high tides, links is surrounded by water and you must walk in to the 1st tee on the dike. Sailboats on both sides. Shore-birds of all kinds. A good test . . . Played Huntercombe. A real good park course. Takes a deal of local knowledge. Fine greens. . . . Finally achieved the ultimate, a day at St. George's. Typical old farmhouse clubhouse. Great links, but not as good as Muirfield.

Dad, via his travels and his golf tournament, befriended an acclaimed English golf writer, Pat Ward-Thomas, who invited him once to play his home course, Royal West Norfolk Golf Club, or, as it was often called, Brancaster. Ward-Thomas took note of Dad's appreciation for golf and wrote about it in his anthology of golf stories *The Lay of the Land*:

> By most standards the clubhouse at Brancaster is a spartan place, existing solely for the purposes of playing golf and providing essential sustenance . . . I had no thought of apology in mind, knowing that Bing, a devoted Anglophile, appreciated the simple values of British golf. He loved the game for its intrinsic merits and not for the rewards it might bring or for the publicity sought by lesser members of his calling.
>
> Whenever, or wherever, one played with him . . . one was soon aware of the quiet pleasure he look in amiable talk, gentle ribbing with his friends, and chatting afterwards over a few "potables" as he called them. There was nothing of the legendary star of show business about Crosby the golfer, either on the course or, for that matter, off it. His manner towards anyone, however humble or exalted their status, was always constant.

Ward-Thomas had captured the essence of my father, recognizing both his genuine passion for the game, as well as how he comported himself, on and off the golf course.

Dad's love of all things British spilled into our home life, too. When he and my mother were searching for domestic help, they hired a proper English butler, Alan Fisher, and his wife, Norma. They came with impeccable credentials; virtually from birth they had been groomed to be domestics for Britain's royal family. They were still children when they began training and working at Buckingham Palace, and eventually became the valet team for the Duke and Duchess of Windsor. The Duke had been King Edward the Eighth, until abdicating his throne to marry American socialite Wallis Simpson, their story popularized in the film *The King's Speech*.

It was not easy convincing Alan and Norma to come to the U.S. to work for my parents. "I'd lived among Van Dykes and Vermeers practically all my life," he said of the works of the renowned artists that adorned the walls of his employers. "I had worked for a Scottish duke who had his own private Leonardo da Vinci. So what did an entertainer have to offer me? When you've worked for the Duke of Windsor, you're not going to impress me if you're Rock Hudson or Carol Burnett."

The Fishers were with us the first sixteen years of my life. After Dad died, Alan and Norma returned to England and began working for Prince Charles and Princess Diana. One day, Alan overheard Diana angrily criticizing a girl of fourteen, who was serving an apprenticeship. "Your Royal Highness, if you please, I would ask that you direct your constructive criticisms to me so that I can reprimand and correct the young lady," Alan said. Princess Diana, who was aware of his fondness for Mom, became irate. "Alan," she said, "it's always been about Kathryn Crosby. You love her, and you've never loved me." Alan replied, "Your Royal Highness, may I say, you will never be the lady that Kathryn Crosby is and she will never be the actress that you are."

\*   \*   \*

IN 1976, MY FATHER WAS IN THE MIDST OF A TOUR CELebrating his fifty years in show business and scheduled a two-week stint at the Palladium in London as well as other sites in Europe. He brought us along with him, and the British media was waiting for us as we deplaned in London. I was asked what I like to do.

"Well, I like to play golf," I said.

They asked whether I might play professionally one day.

Before I could answer, Dad interjected. "No, but I think he'll be a good amateur," he said.

"What are you talking about, Dad?" I replied. "I'm going to be a golf pro."

"Oh, well. The kid can speak for himself."

The *Bing Crosby and Friends* shows at the Palladium were overwhelmingly well received. Rosemary Clooney, who starred alongside Dad in the film *White Christmas*, was part of the show. So were we. Ray Coleman, noted chronicler of all things Beatles and the editor-in-chief of the British publication *Melody Maker*, offered this review of the shows:

> Crosby's edict has always been that the song's the thing, and he has rarely sought to print his personality on the words, which invariably stand up. Seeing him revive these standards, injecting them with a real freshness, was to understand again the power of simplicity in popular song . . .
>
> A magical show then, with dignity and a delightful self-effacing stance, Crosby in his first London concerts

during 50 years of music-making is astonishingly agile and making more history.

Bing at the Palladium—for charity incidentally—will rank as one of the highlights of this or any year. He marked our lives and is demonstrating he still has it. Some say, nostalgia isn't what it used to be. Not so—in disciplined hands it can be richly rewarding.

Then there was this review in the *Express*, which is amusing given the advantage of hindsight:

At the age of 72, Bing Crosby packs the London Palladium. Night after night audiences rise to their feet in tribute to his genius. It could not happen to a nicer person. For Bing is not just a great singer who has brought sunshine and happiness into the lives of millions. He is a good man. Modest and gentle and unassuming. I applaud his triumph. Will people be queuing to see Mick Jagger in the year 2015?

Even though I was in my early teens, I found these shows, and those he would do in New York for a couple of weeks later in the year and another stint in London the following year, fascinating. They represented a mini-comeback of sorts for my father, who in his seventies was selling out the theaters every night. I found that exceedingly cool. It was at these shows that I first began to understand his connection with the public and to gain a respect for his music.

We spent most of the summer of 1976 in Europe, and obviously there was ample golf involved. Some of it was courtesy of the legendary golf promoter Fred Corcoran, who was helping establish the pro-am as a charitable entity on the fledgling PGA European Tour and had enlisted my father's help. (I later became a beneficiary of Corcoran's efforts; for three years I was a card-carrying member of the European Tour.)

Corcoran was a renowned promoter who had worked with Ty Cobb, Babe Ruth, and Ted Williams, among others, and organized most of Dad's War Bond exhibitions and knew how and when to ask Dad for help promoting events.

One such event was a pro-am hosted by Christy O'Connor Sr. as part of the Irish Open week. Dad was part of the pro-am awards ceremony, and he was dazzled by the crystal trophies. "These are beautiful," he said. "I've got to get some of these for our tournament." The trophies were manufactured by an Irish company, Waterford Crystal. Dad immediately commissioned a set and awarded them as trophies to the winners of his own tournament in 1977, the first tournament to do so in America. The following year, he ordered Waterford Crystal trophies for everyone who finished in the top twenty. Then he decided everyone who made the cut should get Waterford Crystal trophies. Waterford Crystal chairman Colm O'Connell was soon playing in the Crosby and would do so for fifteen years or so. Waterford quickly began doing $20 million or more of business in the U.S., and Waterford Crystal trophies became a staple of professional and amateur golf tournaments there. And it all began with my father's participation in the Irish Open pro-am.

Following the Irish Open pro-am, Dad and his troupe performed two shows at the Gaiety Theater in Dublin. For one of those shows, Rosemary Clooney unwittingly wore an orange dress that potentially was a problem. This was during the "Troubles" in Ireland, in which the Orange Order, a Protestant fraternal group from Northern Ireland, often clashed violently with Irish Catholics. It was the only potential misstep of the trip.

On this same trip, we played in the American Express Pro-Am at Frankfurt Golf Club in Germany, a prelude to the German Open there. My brother Harry drew the future legend, Seve Ballesteros, nineteen at the time, as his partner. Dad played with Spanish pro Angel Gallardo, and I played with South African pro Hugh Baiocchi. (I would duel against him some years later in the Portuguese Open when he finished second and I finished third, one and two shots back of Warren Humphries, respectively.)

We then returned to England, where I played in the British Boys Amateur Championship at Sunningdale. I played well, too, with my father in the gallery, watching, as he usually did, from a couple of fairways away.

Then it was on to Scotland for the International Pro-Celebrity, a made-for-television competition involving teams of celebrities and professional golfers from the U.S. against a British team. Dad captained the U.S. team, while Sean Connery was the captain of the Brits. Johnny Miller and Tony Jacklin were the pros involved.

The event was run by Ken Bowden, a prolific author and golf magazine editor, who timidly asked my father to tape an introduction to the show. Dad agreed, and when he showed up at the appointed hour on a chilly morning, he "amiably greeted the crew," Bowden wrote in one of his books, "then turned to me. 'Okay. Script?' "

Bowden handed him the text, at least a few hundred words long, he estimated, and asked whether he should load it into the teleprompter. "Give me a minute," my father said. He stepped away and quietly read it three times. "I got the impression he was trying to memorize it," Bowden wrote, "but couldn't believe that was possible in so short a time."

He returned the script to Bowden, stood in the designated place in front of the camera, and said, "Let's go." Bowden again offered to put it on the teleprompter to let him rehearse once. "Not necessary," Dad said. Bowden, meanwhile, was concerned that Dad would stray from the script. The opposite occurred. "Amazingly, Bing's delivery was virtually word-perfect, meaning he'd memorized the darn thing in just three quick readings. By then, I'd worked a few hundred such tapings, some featuring superstar actors. In golfing terms, Bing Crosby had just made them all look like bumbling hackers."

Among those participating in the actual golf were George C. Scott, Efrem Zimbalist Jr., astronaut Alan Shepherd, Burt Lancaster, and me. Dad ran into a problem with Scott, who had not shown up for his morning round. "There was no panic," Sir Terry Wogan of BBC fame wrote in his book *Is It Me?* "George was not known for his time-keeping; indeed, it was suggested that he might be nursing a bit of a hangover, as he had been seen enjoying a post-prandial snifter or several the evening before."

A search party went looking for him, in his bedroom, the breakfast room, even the bar. He was found at the latter, on the floor, sound asleep and surrounded by empty bottles. He resisted attempts to be moved. Finally, Dad was sent in.

"George, George," he said

Scott finally came to. "Yeah, Bing?"

Dad asked him if he needed anything.

"Two things, Bing," he replied. "A piss and a plane ticket outta here."

Scott soon left for Edinburgh. "Peter Alliss recalls him hurling his golf clubs out the limousine window, as it made its stately progress down the drive," Wogan wrote.

Dad and Phil Harris, meanwhile, had made a side trip from Gleneagles to St. Andrews, a fifty-mile drive, to play thirty-six holes. Afterwards, they had dinner, then set off on the drive back to Gleneagles. Sometime around midnight, they passed a large distillery that clearly was a twenty-four-hour operation, given the number of cars in the parking lot and the smoke coming from the smokestacks.

"Look, Phil, they're making it faster than you can drink it," Dad said.

"Yeah," Harris replied, "but I've got 'em working nights."

Alliss, who would soon become the voice of golf on the BBC and contributor on ABC golf telecasts in the U.S., was the on-camera host for the event, and in his autobiography he wrote about his experience with my father:

> How could one ever forget a week with the late Bing Crosby? At that time he was not too strong, frail, aging. He

was an entirely pleasant man, steeped of course in show business . . . He was a good conversationalist, enjoyed his life, loved the game of golf, loved the people he found in golf, loved going to Scotland. He enjoyed his Scotch and soda at the end of the day, and did every single thing smoothly and quietly. One thing he said which I cannot forget was that every single day of his life he tried to learn something—a new word, a new phrase, a new thought, a new fact. Just something about life. Pity more of us don't do just that.

The mutual respect Dad and the British had for each other was genuine and enduring. This was evident when the audience at the Palladium shows would begin to sing along to Dad's songs, *Pennies from Heaven* and *I'll Be Home for Christmas* and others, having memorized the lyrics during the war years three decades earlier.

He would stop singing and hold the microphone up to the audience, which responded by singing louder, paying homage to a man who during the war and the years that followed had earned their respect and admiration.

# CHAPTER 6

# CADDIES OR KINGS

There was a bygone time that professional golfers were not allowed in the clubhouse. The great American professional Walter Hagen took it as an affront and reacted accordingly. At the 1920 British Open at Royal Cinque Ports, he arrived in a chauffeur-driven luxury automobile. Hagen, attired in a rumpled tuxedo that presumably he had worn through the night, had the chauffeur stop directly in front of the clubhouse, and changed into his golf shoes there, a personal protest, of sorts, against the aristocrats.

It wasn't that long ago in Palm Beach, Florida, that the working class was frowned upon, that in stuffy aristocratic circles those who weren't direct descendants of the Mayflower were confined to the children's table at dinner. One could be overheard at a Palm Beach society dinner saying, "Gentlemen, there are so few of us left," meaning that true gentlemen were those who never worked but merely inherited their wealth.

This was not my father, notwithstanding the fact that he himself *was* a direct descendant of a *Mayflower* passenger, William Brewster. Dad had a great vocabulary, but "pretentious" was not part of it. When I travel, say, to New York City, I choose a hotel not for its amenities or prestige, but maybe because the best street hot dog vendor in the city is outside its front doors. My father was much the same way. One's standing in the social strata was of no concern to him. He was as comfortable with caddies as he was with kings, a man who could mix and match with the Rockefellers, Vanderbilts, and Mellons, as well as caddies and railbirds likely to be betting their dinner money on their next favorite horse.

My godparents reflect the diversity of my parents' friends. Jackie Burke Jr., a golfer (albeit a renowned one, the winner of the Masters and the PGA Championship in 1956), is my godfather; and Nini Martin, high-society personified and a direct descendent of the families that founded San Francisco, is my godmother.

In 1946, Win Rockefeller, son of John D. Rockeller Jr. and a future governor of Arkansas, came up with an idea to host a New Year's Eve party at his grandfather's estate outside Tarrytown, New York. "You bring your gang from show business and I'll bring my friends," Rockefeller said to my father.

"Hmm, but your gang hasn't been exposed to my gang," my father replied.

The gang my father assembled included the comedian Phil Silvers and Rags Ragland, a comedian and character actor who came to fame via burlesque. Dad characterized him as "magna cum laude" in burlesque.

En route, Dad demanded they be on their best behavior with the high-society types with whom they would be partying, a request that proved futile from the moment they arrived at the estate. Barney Dean, a future scriptwriter for the Hope and Crosby *Road* films, told Rockefeller at the door that he could not go any farther because he had forgotten to bring his library card.

Dad glared at him, but the tenor of the evening had been established. Once the groups began partaking of the "flowing bowl," as Dad called the alcohol, singing and dancing followed.

"As long as a person was bright or amusing or congenial, it mattered little to Crosby how wealthy or socially prominent he might be, and his friends included studio technicians, musicians, chauffeurs, horse trainers, and proprietors of bowling alleys," Herbert Warren Wind wrote in *The New Yorker*.

On the wealthy front was George Coleman, my father's best friend. Coleman was an Oklahoma oilman among other varied financial interests and an avid golfer, who counted Ben Hogan among his closest friends in golf, as did my father. The original Mrs. Coleman once was heard saying to her husband, "You're not going to invite any of those golf pro friends of yours to our party tomorrow night, are you?" The future ex-Mrs. Coleman was the antithesis of my father, and she was forever dubbed "the former beloved" by Coleman after they divorced.

Dad's nephew, Howard Crosby, told an illuminating story about my father's lack of what the British journalist Alistair Cooke called "prima donnaism." It occurred in 1975, a few days before the contestants in the Bing Crosby National Pro-Am were set to arrive. "Uncle Bing showed up in town and called to see if I wanted to meet him at Cypress [Point] for a bit of golf the next day," Howard said. "Of course I was up for that, so we planned to meet at the pro shop at 7:30 the next morning. When I got there, Uncle Bing was already sitting on the trunk of his car, changing into his golf shoes. Then he asked the assistant pro if there were any caddies who could play a bit. And [the assistant pro] said there were a couple of single-digit handicappers back there. So Bing hired the two kids to fill out a foursome, plus two more to carry bags, and away we went. I remember thinking at the time that there were undoubtedly hundreds of the wealthiest, most prominent citizens of Carmel/Pebble Beach who would have loved to be in that foursome with Bing Crosby, and here he goes and hires a couple of caddies. How typical of Bing."

Dad's principal playground during his years in Los Angeles was Lakeside Golf Club, an entertainment industry enclave then and now: from Oliver Hardy, W.C. Fields, Johnny Weissmuller, and Gene Autry in the past; and now to Jack Nicholson, Sylvester Stallone, Justin Timberlake, Adam Levine, George Lopez, and Bruce Willis. The coed grillroom was a veritable roundtable for the Hollywood gods.

The club was conveniently located around the corner from Universal Studios, allowing him to play early in the morning and, during summer months, late in the afternoon, often with Bob Hope.

Many days, Dad played a morning round and went to the racetrack in the afternoon. When asked by his playing partners if he wanted to go to the track with them, he invariably would answer, "I have a previous engagement, but I'll see you there."

He then would arrive at the track accompanied by the caddies who had worked his foursome that morning. Inevitably, Dad would overpay each of them by twenty dollars as seed money for their wagers.

He enjoyed playing golf with the club's caddies, too. "People ask me how much golf I've played and how I learned my golf," Dad said. "I learned it playing with these caddies, mostly, and watching pros play." Dad often went to the caddies' rooming house and rousted a few of them to play a one-dollar Nassau (one dollar wagered on the front nine, one dollar on the back, and one on the eighteen holes). Norman Blackburn, in his book *Lakeside Golf Club of Hollywood, 50th Anniversary Book,* wrote that "Bing would rather win a buck from a caddie than a thousand from Dan Topping (the owner of the New York Yankees), which he did many times."

Dad was involved in a famous match with a notorious and mysterious Lakeside member. His name was LaVerne Moore, though he had taken the name John Montague, or "Mysterious Montague," as he came to be known because of his clandestine nature. He was a very good golfer, one of the best in the country, according to legendary sportswriter Grantland Rice. Montague fell in with the Hollywood crowd, even living for a time with Oliver Hardy of Laurel and Hardy fame. One day, Montague defeated my father in a match at Lakeside. Afterwards, in the clubhouse bar, my father complained that he hadn't been given enough strokes.

"I could beat you with a shovel, a bat, and a rake," Montague replied.

"For how much?" Dad asked.

"For five dollars a hole."

That was how it widely has been reported, but I've heard that the bet was for $5,000 a hole, a tidy sum among the well-heeled even today, but more so in those days.

They repaired to the first hole. Montague used a fungo bat off the tee and drove the ball into a bunker. From there, he took a shovel and scooped the ball onto the green about two feet from the hole. He made the putt by using the rake like a pool cue.

"I was history," Dad said.

The mystery surrounding Montague turned out to be the questionable past from which he was hiding. A story with photos on Montague, as his legend grew, appeared in *Time* magazine, piquing the interest of a New York law enforcement official who had spent seven years working on a criminal case involving armed robbery and assault in upstate New York. Montague was arrested for the crimes, though later was acquitted of them.

As for Dad's association with kings (or former kings), one was a golf partner, the Duke of Windsor, formerly King Edward VIII, who had abdicated his throne to marry an American socialite and divorcee, Wallace Simpson. On a visit to Paris one year, Dad teamed with a friend, Ray Graham, in a match with the Duke and Chris Dunphy, the chairman of Seminole Golf Club and one of Dad's friends. The Duke was notorious for his aversion to wagering any more than a few dollars. So neither Dunphy nor Dad bothered to tell him what the bet was that day. Yet every hole or two, either Dunphy or Dad would holler, "Texas." Curious, the Duke asked Dunphy why they were always talking about Texas.

"Never mind," Dunphy said. "I'll explain later."

He waited until the end of the round to tell him. "Every time Bing or I said 'Texas,' that meant we were doubling the bets."

"I say, Chris," the Duke replied, "I'm glad you didn't tell me about it at the time."

Dad's assessment of the Duke's game? "You've got to watch him on a golf course. He always hits his second ball first, and there you are walking down the fairway thinking he's already hit and—whoosh—his other shot comes flying past your head."

Dad mixed comfortably with England's royal family as well. In the summer of 1976, we spent a couple of weeks at Petworth Mansion outside of London. Dad was doing recordings, and I was able to hit practice balls in the vast acreage that surrounded the estate.

During our stay there the entire royal family—Her Royal Highness Queen Elizabeth, Prince Charles, Prince Phillip, and other notables—held a party with us, presumably to showcase their renowned houseguest. Meanwhile, Mom had instructed me to bow when I met the queen, but I thought she was kidding. Alas, I failed to make the gesture in a timely manner, resulting in a stern lecture in royal family etiquette from my mother.

For my mom, being from West Columbia, Texas, meeting the royals and, better yet, spending time with them was a personal achievement. So a few weeks later when we were attending the races at the Goodwood Racecourse, Queen Elizabeth was there, too. Her Royal Highness sent an emissary down to invite us to the Royal Enclosure, or Royal Box, as Americans might call it. Mom was thrilled at the invitation, Dad less so.

He repeatedly declined, citing the fact he was underdressed for the occasion. Top hat and tails generally are required for gentlemen in the Royal Enclosure, and Dad had a green plaid sport jacket that he wore far too often in his later years. The queen insisted that it didn't matter, but Dad continued to decline. In his defense, he was color-blind, and as I recall was wearing brown shoes with one red sock and one green sock. Mom, meanwhile, seethed at the missed opportunity.

Presidents were also playing partners of my father's, among them President John F. Kennedy, with whom he played thirteen holes at Palm Beach Country Club in April of 1961. "The president has a good-looking golf swing," my father said. "It's smooth. All the fundamentals are right. He has a good stance and grip and slow backswing. He hits the ball with determination. He's out there 240 or 250 yards." Dad partnered with the president in a match against Kennedy's father, Joseph, and Chris Dunphy.

One of the legendary stories included Dunphy's failing to concede Kennedy's three-foot putt for par on the first hole, despite the president's plea to do so.

"Make a pass at it," Dunphy said. "I want to see your stroke."

"I work in the Oval Office all day for citizens like you," Kennedy replied. "And now you're not going to give me this putt?"

Dunphy said nothing.

"OK," Kennedy said. "But let's keep moving. I've got an appointment after we finish with the director of the Internal Revenue."

"Putt's good," Dunphy said. "Pick it up."

Dad said the best part of Kennedy's game was how he would arrange matches on the first tee. "He'll only bet a dollar or two. But an awful lot of negotiation goes on before the clubs start swinging. He works out the best possible arrangement before he makes a move. It gives me confidence that he'll be able to handle those international rascals."

About those international rascals: After his abbreviated round with the president, Dad recounted the day to my mother. "He told me that during the round special agents came up to the president," Mom said. "They had a little conversation. Turns out that was the day of the kidnapping threat against Caroline." The president's daughter, three at the time, was staying at the nearby oceanfront home of her grandparents Joseph and Rose Kennedy and reportedly was the target of pro–Fidel Castro Cubans.

My father developed a friendship with President Kennedy, though he did not use his status to seek out these kinds of relationships. Basking in reflected glory was not part of his repertoire. These relationships always evolved through a mutual interest in golf. When President Kennedy was planning a weekend retreat in the Palm Springs, California, area in 1962, he was invited to stay at Frank Sinatra's house in Rancho Mirage, but chose to stay at my father's home instead. At the time, Kennedy's brother Robert F. Kennedy, the attorney general, was investigating organized crime figures and the president balked at staying at the home of a man thought to have connections with those under investigation. Sinatra reportedly was livid. He had built a helicopter pad and a guest wing on the house for the occasion. And when he discovered the president would be staying at my father's house, he said, "Staying with Bing Crosby? He's not even a Democrat."

A long-standing rumor, incidentally, was that Kennedy had a visitor during his stay at my father's house. Her name: Marilyn Monroe. Kennedy, incidentally, stayed at Dad's house on three occasions, the last time a month before his assassination.

Dad, meanwhile, valued each friend he acquired with an equal priority, never valuing one over the other because of his or her station in life. If there was an agenda, it was to spend time with the people that he had the most fun with, be it a fellow entertainer, a famous golfer, a business tycoon, a caddy, a scriptwriter, or even the royal family, with whom he had a bond based on their unspoken understanding that together they had been the backbone of boosting morale among troops and Allied leaders in those dark and uncertain times.

# CHAPTER 7

# HOGAN AND THE INCREDIBLE MATCH

When I was about twelve years old, I was having dinner with my mom and dad and Dad's friend Jackie Burke at the Del Monte Lodge during a Crosby tournament when Jackie dominated the dinner conversation. He was talking about how the vast majority of golfers were playing winter rules year-round and how wrong that was. I could clearly detect Mom was having second thoughts about having married an avid golfer who had professional golfers as friends, all of whom talk about the rules of golf at dinner.

But this was my father's passion, and golfers, professionals, and amateurs alike were among his closest friends. It has been my good fortune that many of them became my friends and acquaintances as well, and in some cases close friends and a part of my day-to-day life at different points.

George Coleman was probably my father's best friend, while Ben Hogan, one of the top three or four players in history, was one of his closest friends from golf. Hogan and Coleman were paired together in an early Crosby Clambake, resulting in a lifelong friendship as well. Coleman was a pilot who would fly Hogan from tournament to tournament in the Pennzoil corporate jet. On two occasions, they experienced an engine failure in mid-flight. On the second occasion, Hogan said, "George, you couldn't have possibly blown another engine, did you?"

George admitted the engine had failed, but declared that it wasn't his responsibility to oversee engine repairs. Hogan found the answer insufficient, but the plane landed safely; they remained friends, and Hogan continued his assault on golf history.

Hogan's friendship with Coleman allowed him to spend a couple weeks at Seminole to prepare for the Masters each year and actually find reasonable competition from the membership. Rumor had it that one member, Bob Sweeney, actually would give Hogan a shot a side in their matches the first two days he was there, then would play even during the rest of his stay. Considering that only Sam Snead and Byron Nelson would have been considered equals in those days, that's a strong testament to Sweeney's game.

After Hogan nearly lost his life in an accident on a Texas highway, his rehabilitation in part included taking his wife Valerie dancing most every night. He became quite adept at the fox-trot. Coleman once told me, however, that this infuriated Valerie, because she knew why she was being courted well into their marriage—so that Hogan could strengthen his legs in an attempt to return to professional golf as fast as possible. Finally, she gave in and simply imagined that it was her husband trying to court her all over again.

Dad not only played golf with both Hogan and Coleman, but he hunted with them as well. One year, Dad invited Hogan and another popular tour pro, Jimmy Demaret, to hunt with him for a few weeks at his ranch in Elko, Nevada. Hogan and Demaret were friends, both native Texans, but they had conflicting personalities.

"Demaret is swashbuckling, ebullient, a gay blade of the fairways," Dad wrote. "Hogan is dour, taciturn, serious, and intense."

At one point, they were hunting at an elevation approaching 9,000 feet. Hogan spotted a deer across a gorge and fired, hitting and dropping it. It took them nearly an hour to navigate the gorge to get to the fallen animal. When they finally arrived, the deer was gone, leaving behind a quantity of blood.

"Well, I guess you didn't hit him," Demaret said, aiming the needle at his favorite target, a man he called "Blueblades" for his habit of grinding his teeth at night.

"Of course I hit him," Hogan replied. "Didn't I?"

"Yes," my father said. "I thought I heard the bullet hit and the deer certainly went down."

"I think he just tripped," Demaret said.

"Tripped?" Hogan replied. "How about the blood all over the snow?"

"The high altitude got him," Demaret said. "He had a nosebleed."

So it went with this odd couple.

I was fortunate to know both Coleman and Hogan. After Dad died, Coleman became one of my great friends. He was a bona fide boomer from Miami, Oklahoma, whose father and uncle had staked a land claim when Oklahoma was opened for settlement. As luck would have it, their swath of land was loaded with lead and zinc deposits.

Coleman, who was twenty-one when his father died, began diversifying the family holdings. He placed one bet on an up-start oil drilling company, which eventually became Pennzoil. He was a man about whom it was said owned 5 percent of every-thing. He was an executive in a lead and zinc mining company and a truck manufacturing company. He was a director on the board of the Pennzoil Company for thirty-three years. He was chairman and president of the First National Bank in Miami and a board member of Flo-Sun Incorporated, the Detroit Ti-gers, Chris Craft Industries, and the Ben Hogan Company.

A friend once said that although he wasn't the wealthiest man in the world, no king, pharaoh, or prince ever enjoyed a better life. Coleman owned a palatial mansion on the ocean in Juno Beach, Florida, and a summer retreat at Castle Pines south of Denver. Each year, he'd rent a house in Pebble Beach for two to four months, lease a house for part of the summer on the Amalfi coast in Italy, and lease a 20,000-square-foot ocean-view house in April and May in Baja, California, to deep-sea fish with Dad and me. And he was an avid and tal-ented golfer, a past champion of the Oklahoma State Amateur, as well as a member of Augusta National Golf Club and Semi-nole Golf Club, the latter of which he was president.

Late in 1978, Coleman and his wife, Dawn, invited me to stay at the Colemans' home in Juno Beach with Ben Hogan and his wife, Valerie, to play golf at Seminole for four days. Contrary to reputation, Hogan was a charming man in social situations, including those involving the Palm Beach set. He was delightful to every guest Coleman would invite to his society dinner parties. At one such party, I recall Hogan, cigarette holder in hand, introducing himself to a lady socialite.

"Hello, I'm Ben Hogan," he said.

"Why, yes you are," she replied, while failing to recall her own name to complete the introduction.

I had just read Arnold Palmer's book *Go For Broke*, which goes into great detail about the U.S. Open that Palmer won at Cherry Hills Country Club in Denver in 1960. Hogan was vying to win the Open for a record fifth time; he was tied for the lead when he came to the par-five seventeenth hole in the final round, and had a fifty-five-yard third shot over water to a pin set near the front of the green. "He lobbed a soft pitch that was just too short, two feet too short," Herbert Warren Wind wrote. The ball rolled back into the water, "and his stirring bid for his fifth Open title was over."

One night at dinner during my stay, I naively asked Hogan what he remembered about that shot. Mrs. Hogan cringed. "Oh, no, you can't ask him about that shot," she said. "He still has nightmares about it." Coleman, meanwhile, grinned like a Cheshire cat, enjoying seeing his friend put on the spot. Yet Hogan answered graciously. "Nathaniel, I hit it exactly the way I wanted," he said. "The greens were as firm as a rock, so for me to hit it close I had to land it short of the pin. The ball landed just where I wanted, but instead of hopping forward it hit a soft spot in the green and spun back into the water. I couldn't believe it. I still can't."

Years later, in an interview with Ken Venturi, he described the shot and said, "It's something I think about every day and it rips my guts out."

On the final day of my stay at the Colemans, I packed my bags, put them in the car, and we headed to the club for one last round. When we arrived, we began taking our shoes from the trunk when Mr. Hogan spotted a large hair dryer.

"What's this?" he asked.

"Well, that's a hair dryer, Mr. Hogan," I said.

"Whose is it?"

This was 1978, when long hair was *de rigueur* for those of my generation and many of us were using hair dryers.

"Well," I said sheepishly, "it's mine, Mr. Hogan."

He examined it, a puzzled look on his face.

"But hair dryers are for girls," he replied. I was mortified.

I had written to the Hogans after that visit, not to defend my use of the hair dryer but to tell them how elated I was to have spent time with them. I had used Bing Crosby National Pro-Am Golf Championship letterhead that had my name on it, as the heir to my father's role in running the tournament. The letter was dated January 12, 1979:

> *Dear Mr. and Mrs. Hogan:*
> *I wanted to take this chance to tell you how much I enjoyed meeting both of you this New Year's.*

*The Colemans, who have been very close to our family
for some time, make occasions such as New Year's very
special. However, this was an occasion I do not think
I will ever forget (although I would like to forget how I
played).*

*Having played with you, Mr. Hogan, I feel I have
learned from analyzing your swing and method of
concentration. Meeting you, Mrs. Hogan, was also a real
pleasure and I think I will take your advice and avoid the
ski slopes in the future.*

*Meeting you both has been very pleasurable for me, not
only because you are friends of the Colemans and were
friends of my father's, but because you are such fine people
and provide an example that I will try to follow.*

*Best wishes for the New Year.*

*Nathaniel*

In the 1982 NCAAs and other tournaments that year, I
actually played with a set of Ben Hogan's personal golf clubs,
original grips, that I had found in George Coleman's garage.
Every time Hogan would change out his set of clubs, his old
ones would wind up in Coleman's garage. I played a California
State Amateur with one of Hogan's fairway woods, with the
same grip. I had a set of his personal irons that I used in the
NCAA Championship at Pinehurst. I played most of that year
with those irons.

I HAD KNOWN COLEMAN FOR MOST OF MY LIFE. HE WAS
there when Dad took us to the Olympics in Munich in 1972,

when I was still in my autograph-collecting stage. Two autographs that I recall getting there were from the great American distance runner Steve Prefontaine and the legendary sprinter Jesse Owens.

Coleman once told a story about a standing game he, Lawson Little, Francis Brown, and my father had at Cypress Point. Francis Brown was a wealthy Hawaiian, the founder of the Mauni Lani Resort on the Big Island, and an excellent golfer, who had a home in Pebble Beach. He also was a character. He was said to have arrived in the States to play in the 1929 U.S. Amateur at Pebble Beach with a marching band in tow. The band was to begin playing as he completed each round. In a qualifying round, Francis, it turned out, was held up by a ruling in the foursome in front of him and was invited in for a drink from the homeowners of the house opposite the fourteenth tee. Although Francis was in a solid position to qualify and advance to match play, he did not emerge from the house for two days. The marching band played without him in wonderment.

Dad carved September and October out of his recording schedule for golf at Cypress Point with this trio. Their ritual: a big buffet lunch, eighteen holes, shots of bourbon. Coleman and my father would have four or five shots of the bourbon to be sociable. Little, who won two U.S. Amateurs and a U.S. Open, would drop out after fifteen to twenty shots. Brown, meanwhile, would show off by having another fifteen or twenty shots. He'd sleep it off the next morning, and then they'd start over again at lunch and do this every day for six to eight weeks.

I enrolled at the University of Miami in Florida partially because Coleman lived only two hours away, in Palm Beach, and it was a foregone conclusion that I would be able to play Seminole Golf Club every weekend as his guest.

Jill, my steady girlfriend at the time, received an academic scholarship and joined me at the university. For the first dinner engagement I had with Coleman, I had to tell Jill that she had to eat at a diner and to wait for me until the dinner party had ended, some three hours later. No, I was not a terrific boyfriend, and she eventually dumped me.

At any rate, Coleman heard about this and insisted Jill and I come to dinner together the following night. Coleman, sixty-seven at the time, met her and was smitten. He stopped talking about Bo Derek, the hot model/movie star, and began directing his attention towards Jill. George and Alan Ryan, the president of Seminole Golf Club, then began conspiring and placing Jill between them at all future dinner parties. I'd be seated at the far end of the table next to widows and women who wished they were widows, all in their seventies and eighties. Jill enjoyed what she thought was harmless attention as the old codgers dropped their napkins next to her in hopes that she would lean over in her low-cut blouse.

Even with the shenanigans it was protocol when it came to separate bedrooms. Jill was staged in the basement headquarters, which were really tricked out and nice. I was upstairs in the guest room some eighty feet away. On our first stay with this arrangement, George painstakingly told me exactly how not to trigger the alarm should I "need a drink or something from the basement." He was, as they say today, "an enabler."

Today, I am a great friend with Tad Ryan, Alan Ryan's grandson, who is a few years older than me. I was at a party with him recently, and his twenty-year-old daughter Mimi was there as well. When I got a chance to talk with her, I recounted the Coleman dinner party situation and asked her if she realized her great grandfather used to hit on my girlfriend. That's covering several generations.

George had a great sense of humor and would constantly have the needle out and ready, a trait I've adapted into my own personality, to the dismay of my "current wife" (as I call her) and others who fail to understand the humor. George would go so far as to send postcards from Europe to married friends. On the front of the postcards might be a topless model on the beach in the south of France. He'd have his secretary or any other willing accomplice write a love note and seal it with a lipstick smear. George loved a good prank. It took his circle of friends a while to catch on and must have caused some marital strife.

The time I got to spend with Coleman was priceless. The stories he could tell, too. Among those I frequently heard at dinner parties was that of a match played at the Cypress Point Club: Hogan and Byron Nelson, hall of famers on the back nine of their careers, versus two upstart amateurs, Harvie Ward and Ken Venturi. It was a relatively obscure story until writer Mark Frost, an avid golfer best known as the co-creator of the television series *Twin Peaks*, wrote a book about it entitled *The Match*.

In 1956, the group was assembled in Pebble Beach for the Bing Crosby Pro-Am. Coleman held a cocktail party early in the week, and Eddie Lowery was there. Lowery was an automobile dealer in the Bay Area who was better known as the eleven-year-old who caddied for Francis Ouimet when he famously won the U.S. Open at the Country Club at Brookline in 1913 (also recounted in a book by Mark Frost, *The Greatest Game Ever Played*).

Lowery had accepted several cocktails offered by Coleman's Italian butler, Franco (who, incidentally, introduced me to my first daiquiri when I was eleven). Lowery began boasting that a pair of amateurs who worked for him at the car dealership were peaking and that one of them likely was going to win the Masters or the U.S. Open that year. He also boldly said no two golfers anywhere could beat them head-to-head in a best-ball match.

"Anyone, pros included?" Coleman asked.

"Pros included," Lowery replied.

Coleman then phoned Hogan and explained the situation and asked whether he'd be amenable to teaming with Byron Nelson to teach Lowery a lesson while simultaneously lightening his wallet. Hogan agreed, as did Nelson. The match was on.

The quality of golf made it a match of legend: Hogan shot 63, Venturi 65, and Nelson and Ward 67s. The four of them combined to make twenty-seven birdies and an eagle. All bets were forgiven in homage to the memorable display of talent.

Harvie Ward later became a great friend. I remember seeing him on the cover of *Golf World* magazine in the early 1970s and asking my father about him. Dad said he was a good friend of his, though I did not meet him until after Dad died. Bob Roos, who helped my father with his tournament pairings, said to me, "I know you want to hang out with your Dad's old buddies, so you've got to meet Harvie Ward.

Here's how Roos described him to me: "Harvie was such a great player, but he loved women, and they loved him. It was so bad that if Harvie had a one-foot putt to win the U.S. Open and a pretty girl in the gallery winked at him, he'd forget to hit the putt."

In the mid-1950s Harvie was one of the best players in the world, though he was an amateur. In 1955, he tied for eighth in the Masters, tied for seventh in the U.S. Open, and won the U.S. Amateur, the first of two consecutive Amateurs he won. He also had won a British Amateur and an NCAA championship.

Ward, the last of the great career amateurs, was determined in 1957 to become the first player ever to win the U.S. Amateur three straight years. Alas, he was stripped of his amateur status when the United States Golf Association discovered that through his job at Lowery's auto dealership he had had his golf travel expenses paid for. He never again competed at a high level and eventually turned pro and took a number of club jobs.

I began playing practice rounds with Harvie before the Bing Crosby National Pro-Am in 1978, and because our personalities suited each other we hit it off from the beginning. When I went to North Carolina to play in the North & South Amateur Championship in Pinehurst, he was the director of golf there and I stayed with him, sealing the bond of another generational friendship.

Harvie was one of the great characters. The best story involving Dad and Harvie occurred during the French Open in 1953 in which both were playing. They had rented a Mercedes convertible and had met a couple of models. After midnight, they parked their car in front of their hotel, at which point Dad began serenading the ladies with love songs, while Harvie sat in the back seat looking handsome. It is not known whether the women appreciated the serenade, but a woman from a neighboring apartment building was not amused.

She took her full chamberpot, as old Parisian buildings didn't always have indoor plumbing in those days, and emptied it into the convertible, drenching all of them in urine. Dad slowly turned to Harvie now knowing that any aspirations for the evening with the women would be lost and said, "There's always a critic."

Some three decades later, in 1987, Harvie and his future wife, Joanne, while each was still married to someone else, snuck off to San Francisco and were in the gallery together at the U.S. Open at the Olympic Club in 1987. During the telecast, a television camera zoomed in on them while the broadcasters noted that he was one of the last amateurs to contend in a U.S. Open. Divorces soon followed. Dad's old friend Bob Roos suggested I get my checkbook ready because I was going to have to pay his rent in the interim. I imagined the worst, yet when he picked me up at the Orlando airport after I returned from qualifying at the British Open, he was driving a Jaguar with a vanity license plate that said "HIS." Turns out that his paramour and future wife was from a well-heeled family from the North Shore of Chicago. They soon married and spent eighteen years together until Harvie's death from liver cancer in 2004. I was asked to give the eulogy at the clubhouse in Pinehurst in front of some 500 of Harvie's friends, both new and old.

Venturi, meanwhile, would have a successful professional career that included a victory in the 1964 U.S. Open and later became a fixture on CBS's golf telecasts. He ended up living on the same block we did in Hillsborough. Venturi and his two sons, Matt and Tim, were frequent houseguests of ours. When I hosted the Bing Crosby National Pro-Am, Ken and I were in the broadcast booth together. We reconnected several years later when he had an endorsement contract with Orlimar Golf Company, and I was a partner in the company. He was a big part of our direct response marketing that together with Roger Maltbie helped grow our sales from one million dollars to more than $100 million for two years running.

Hogan had been at Pebble Beach in 1956 only because my father had talked him out of retirement following his devastating loss to Jack Fleck in the U.S. Open in 1955. Hogan was seeking a record fifth U.S. Open victory and appeared to have it won, before a late rally by Fleck tied him and sent it to an eighteen-hole playoff the following day. Fleck shot a 69, Hogan a 72, to record one of the great upsets in golf history.

Afterward, Hogan essentially announced his retirement. "I'm through with serious competitive golf," he told the assembled crowd at the Olympic Club in Daly City, California, that day. "I want to become a weekend golfer. It's too hard to train for a big tournament."

He did not play a tournament the rest of the year. Then he got a phone call from Dad, urging him to come play the Crosby again, using the premise that with him in the field, the crowds would be larger and as a result so would the charitable contributions. Apparently Hogan agreed only if Dad would be his amateur partner. They even took the Pro-Am lead in the first round. "After that, Bing continued to play very well and I played very badly," Hogan said. The final round was marred by Crosby weather—cold and wet. When they got to the thirteenth hole, where Dad had a home adjacent to the fairway, he said to Hogan, "Let's chuck it and go inside for a drink, boy."

"But Ben wouldn't quit," Dad said. "So I couldn't quit, either. Grrrr. Very rugged."

They played on and Hogan shot an 81 and finished nineteen strokes behind tournament winner Dr. Cary Middlecoff. "That house sure looked warm and inviting when we finally made it," Dad said.

Incidentally, it was the last time my father ever played in his own tournament. As for Hogan, he did not retire entirely. He continued to play in the Masters and U.S. Open and assorted other tournaments and won once more, the Colonial National Invitation, the fifth time he won the event.

He also played in the U.S. Open at the Olympic Club in 1966, when he was closing in on his fifty-fourth birthday. Dad went each day, sitting by the green at the third hole, a long par three. Hogan used a two-iron each day and hit his tee shot within ten feet all four rounds and never made birdie. Even at that age, he was better than most with his irons, but his putter by then was his nemesis. Still, he finished twelfth.

Coleman told me once that Hogan was fascinated with watching the great baseball star Ted Williams and attended his games as often as he could, frequently going alone. He'd purchase a ticket as close to the field as possible and would study Williams' swing, one legend observing another legend's mechanics.

I was able to witness Hogan's swing up close during those four days we spent as guests of Coleman. I can recall how well he practiced, even at the age of sixty-five. He was still a reasonably good player, though not near the standard he had once set. Still, his practice sessions were as disciplined and as intense as they ever were. He would choose the far left side of the driving range at Seminole. Generally there would be a right to left wind coming off the ocean. He would hit shots that looked virtually dead straight, but the stiff right to left breeze gave away the fact that he was hitting a relatively hard cut shot.

The Crosby-Coleman-Hogan alliance was a strong one. I was grateful to know and spend time with Hogan, and Coleman and I were friends as if we were the same age. Incidentally, both Coleman and Hogan died the same week in 1997.

# CHAPTER 8

# FAMILY FRIENDS

Ben Hogan, George Coleman, and Harvie Ward were exceptional family friends, spanning generations, for which I'm grateful. And then there is the inimitable Jackie Burke Jr., my godfather.

My earliest recollection of Jackie was when I was four and he came to visit us at our home in Hillsborough. I got excited when Dad told me that Jackie had brought me a birthday gift. I was thinking it was going to be some type of a toy, hopefully a train set. But Jackie had selected a denim sheik jacket, army green. Still, I sported a big smile when I had my photo taken with Jackie and Dad. The photo hangs in my house, my mom's house, and in the locker room at Champions Golf Club in Houston.

Later that year, Jackie sent me an eight-by-ten, black-and-white glossy photo of himself standing in front of the clubhouse at Augusta National. "To my godson Nathaniel," he wrote, "I sure hope to see you playing here at the Masters one day."

Eighteen years later, when I was playing in the Masters for the third time, I decided to return the favor and recruited his daughter Lisa to take a photo of me in front of the Augusta National clubhouse, in the same pose as Jackie. I sent him an eight-by-ten glossy on which I wrote, "To my godfather Jackie, no problem getting here to the Masters, your godson Nathaniel."

Burke was an accomplished player, a winner of sixteen PGA Tour events, including the Masters and the PGA Championship in the same year, 1956. A year later, he and fellow Texan and tour pro Jimmy Demaret founded Champions Golf Club, where more than 500 members have handicaps in the single digits. He was as well one of Dad's closest friends, hence he and my mother assigned Jackie the cumbersome task of being my godfather, or "the responsibility that Bing left me," as Burke often says to audiences.

He also is fond of saying that whatever he advises me to do, I do the opposite. "I told him not to turn pro, that he didn't hit the ball three hundred yards, and that he really wasn't that straight, either. The next thing I know I'm reading in the paper that Crosby turns pro."

Jackie is painfully honest, literally so at times, to which Hal Sutton, the former PGA Championship winner, can attest. Burke was giving a putting lesson to Sutton at Champions one year and asked him to hole 100 consecutive putts from three feet. Sutton was wrestling with the yips at the time and missed six or seven putts in the first couple of minutes. Jackie, meanwhile, was hunched over, hands on knees, as if inspecting Sutton's mechanics, when he unexpectedly punched him in the stomach after a miss. Sutton buckled over. Once he caught his breath, he said, "What on earth did you do that for?"

"Hal, when you miss a short putt, it's got to hurt."

Jackie had no internal filter. He said what he thought, even when he was talking to or about me. Several years ago, Michael Bamberger of *Sports Illustrated* was talking to Burke for a story he was doing on me. Burke told him that I'm a plus-four handicap at talking. Tour golfers have handicaps of plus-four and higher, so apparently I'm tour level at talking. The last time I saw him, he said, "Man, you had better put some distance between you and that fork of yours. I mean just push the plate back a foot or two."

Once not long after he won the Masters, he was sitting next to Bobby Jones, the legendary amateur golfer who founded Augusta National Golf Club and the Masters, at the Champions dinner.

"Mr. Jones, when did you turn pro?" he asked him.

"Jackie, I am not a pro," Jones replied.

"But Mr. Jones, you filmed those Warner Brothers instructional films, right? You received money for those films, right?"

"Sir," Jones replied, "I am an amateur. I am not a pro."

Burke knew that, but was upset that Harvie Ward, one of the best players of their generation even while playing as an amateur, was stripped of his amateur status by the United States Golf Association for accepting travel expenses from his boss, Eddie Lowery, the Bay Area car dealer.

Another PGA Tour star Phil Mickelson once flew out from California to take a putting lesson from Jackie. Mickelson had been troubled by missing short putts under pressure and was told that Jackie could help him.

When Jackie takes on a new student, he takes them into his office for what is tantamount to a papal visit. After going through formalities with Mickelson and his agent, Steve Loy, Jackie asked, "So, Phil, you flew all the way out from California? I mean, you got in a plane and everything, right? Really, all the way from California, like over 1,500 miles, right?"

"Why, yes, Mr. Burke, I did," Mickelson replied.

"And you say that you came all this way for putting lessons, is that right?"

"Yes, Mr. Burke, I heard from many guys that you could help me with my putting." Jackie shook his head.

"You came all this way for putting lessons? I mean, every time I see you on the TV in a tournament you're by a water hazard taking a drop. Don't you want some long-game lessons, too, after flying all this way?"

Steve Elkington, a former PGA Championship winner and close friend of Burke's, has been on the receiving end, too. "Hey, I told Steve Elkington the other day when I caught him buying a leather couch for $10,000 that he was going in the wrong direction and it was going to mess up his career. I asked him, 'What are you doing with that couch? Watch TV all day and have your brain turn to mush? You need some hardback chairs and some classic books. You need to sit and read when you come home off the golf course and not think about relaxing. You need to be in an uncomfortable chair so you can concentrate when you're reading some books every night. You do not need comfort. It will ruin you. You need to be uncomfortable so you can concentrate."

Steve kept the leather couch and missed out on at least forty wins and ten majors, according to Jackie. "Comfort," Jackie would say, "what has comfort ever done for anyone except make them soft?"

When the Hall of Famer Ben Crenshaw was a PGA Tour rookie, his first tournament in his first full season was at the Crosby in 1974. His amateur partner was Dad's friend Virgil Sherrill, and they were paired with Jackie Burke and George Coleman. Ben shot a 77. He had a temper in those days and punched the door of one of the Oldsmobile courtesy cars. Jackie Burke was an eyewitness, but, out of character, chose to say nothing.

The following day I was in Crenshaw's gallery and watched him push a short-iron second shot well right of the first green, leading to a double bogey. He pushed another second shot right and out of bounds at the second hole, resulting in his spearing the turf with his iron.

At this point, Jackie could not resist commenting. "Man, those Oldsmobiles are going to be in trouble tonight," he yelled from across the fairway, loud enough for those in the large gallery to hear. Crenshaw knew he had been had. He had been seen the night before.

When Crenshaw was struggling with his game a few years later, Burke told him, "Ben, I don't know if this is a slump anymore. You really ought to start thinking about doing something else. Man, I know I can get you a job selling cars in Houston if this bad game of yours doesn't change." Not something Crenshaw needed to hear while fighting for pars in the middle of a tournament.

Crenshaw never sold cars. He developed a lifelong tolerance of and love for Jackie, as so many have, and they've been friends for years. He also had nineteen wins on the PGA Tour, including two Masters, and had the burden of being my pro-am partner at the Crosby eight times.

Jackie had an opinion on virtually everything, including players clinging to their careers. "Can you believe these guys playing the tour at thirty-six or thirty-eight years old? I mean, what are they thinking? Lanny Wadkins, I mean, he was a great player, but what is he doing out there at forty? I'll tell you what they're doing out there. These egomaniacs can't let go of the gallery. They can't give up the sound of that applause when they make a putt." That took a little bit of the glamour of playing the Tour away from me.

When I was about twelve, I took my first lesson from Jackie, on the range at the Crosby, in front of the gallery and touring professionals. I was exceedingly nervous, but was hitting the ball as well as I ever had. After eight or ten shots, Jackie said, "Man, the hardest thing about this game for you, boy, is going to be walking." I was on cloud nine.

Jackie loved my father and the two of them enjoyed each other's company. Dad often took Harry and me down to Champions Golf Club in Houston to expose us to Jackie and his wisdom and knowledge of the game, and to Jimmy Demaret, another friend of Dad's and a three-time Masters champion. After Dad died, Burke came out of retirement to play in the Crosby with me as his amateur partner. He had just gone through a tough divorce that he didn't want with his wife of more than twenty years. We had a great time, and it was likely as meaningful for Jackie as it was for me.

I'll never forget Demaret giving Dad a lesson and telling him not to worry about his swing getting flatter, since that should be everyone's tendency as they get older. It's a lesson I've kept in mind now that I'm not as limber as I once was.

After two years of limited success on the European Tour I went to Jackie to revamp my swing. I basically lived with him throughout that winter. He was sixty-four and about to marry a much younger woman and was taking taekwondo lessons every morning at 6:30, after which we'd go to the course for hours of lessons.

He also was lecturing me at breakfast, lunch, and dinner, on golf, life, discipline, politics, business, morals, the Catholic church, and how I should plan and live life for the next sixty years.

"You think someone really cares about that tournament you won years ago?" he said. "You think they'll care about how many tournaments you're going to win one day. I mean, do you think that anyone really cares about the tournaments I won? I mean, do I really hear people saying today, 'Who won that Roman chariot race back in the year 3,000 B.C.?' You don't hear people asking about those chariot races or the gladiator fights, so don't think they care about your win or my win. No one cares. You win for yourself. You are doing this thing for yourself. No one else."

On the way to his wedding to Robin, I was in the car with him, and he was lecturing me about "marginal" commitments, though I had been neither married nor engaged at that time.

"How about these kids that go to the altar with a piece of paper in their hands," he said, speaking of prenuptial agreements. "I mean, can you believe it? They go to the altar and have a piece of paper that says if this doesn't work out 'I get this and you get that.' I mean, that is the essence of a marginal commitment."

I followed his advice and eventually paid full spousal support for quite a while.

On marrying again, to a younger woman, he offered this: "I mean, I tried to date women my age, but if they were single at my age, they'd been through a lot. Hey, it's not their fault, but, man, I don't need that baggage. So I meet this girl. I know she's way too young for me, but she has no baggage. So I start giving her lessons and she's a great player. I mean, I thought to myself, this is someone that could make me happy. So I acted on it. Hey, she's really cute and comes from a great family and I've got her hitting the ball fantastic. And there's no baggage."

Robin Moran Burke, to whom he has been married thirty years, has won two Texas Amateurs, was a runner-up in the U.S. Women's Amateur, and was selected to captain the U.S. Curtis Cup team. They have a twenty-seven-year-old daughter, Meeghan, who is now married. I doubt there was a pre-nup for that marriage.

Jackie didn't like "GOO-roos, " as he called today's teaching professionals. "Man, I see these guys walking up and down the range on the tour, recruiting their next victim. They work with the best touring pros, and I still just don't get it. I mean, I've been in a lot of these teachers' homes and look in their dens and libraries for their hardware and I never see any trophies. How can these tour stars be taking lessons from guys with no trophies?"

On the business front, I went to Houston to set up our distribution there after I had bought the Toney Penna Equipment Company, with the help of billionaire Nelson Doubleday. Jackie gave me a lecture on how to proceed. "Listen, you can't come to my town and cherry pick the best accounts," he said. "If you want to build the Penna brand in this city you need to hit every pro. You don't want to miss one place, and I'll see to it that you don't."

I was calling on the late great Dick Harmon, one of the Harmon brothers renowned for their teaching prowess, who at the time was at River Oaks Country Club. As I was explaining the inherent values of the Toney Penna Cobalt metal woods, Jackie called him.

"Is Nathaniel there?" Jackie said.

"Yes, he's here," Harmon said.

"Is he peddling his wares?"

"Yes."

"Well, are you going to throw him a bone?"

"Yeah, I'm going to throw him a bone."

"Well, that's a relief," Jackie said, "because I heard Nelson Doubleday was down to his last five hundred million."

Jackie is likely to outlive us all. He still runs Champions Golf Club with Robin, and at ninety-three, is still quick-witted and full of knowledge, and still teaching. My son Nathaniel Jr.

took several lessons from him while he attended Tulane University in New Orleans. Jackie began preaching to him about internships and making money, instilling in him that it's all about "self-sufficiency." Nathaniel is twenty-six now and selling insurance. On a recent birthday, his request was for me to go with him to Houston so that he could take another lesson from my ageless godfather.

It was an example of generational friendship at its best.

I MUST HAVE SPENT THOUSANDS OF HOURS WITH TONEY Penna from 1977 until his death in 1994. He was an interesting man, Italian born, the son of a carpenter who was looking to find a better life for his family in the U.S. They came through Ellis Island, when Toney was very young. They settled in Harrison, New York, where he caddied at Green Meadows Country Club.

He became a professional golfer who in 1934 became an emissary for the MacGregor Golf Company and held a prominent position with it for the next thirty-five years. He met the Scottish pro and future U.S. Open champion Tommy Armour, who helped teach him how to make his own golf clubs.

He was an accomplished player, who was simultaneously popular and controversial. On the latter note, he had the MacGregor checkbook and a significant budget to sign players. Among those he signed were Ben Hogan, Byron Nelson, Jackie Burke, Louise Suggs, Jimmy Demaret, and Jack Nicklaus.

In 1969, he left MacGregor and started his own equipment company that produced quality woods used by Lee Trevino,

Tom Watson, Gary Player, and Seve Ballesteros, all of whom won major championships with Penna clubs.

Shortly before he died, Dad introduced Toney to me. He gave me a lesson at the Burlingame Country Club and for the next ten years gave me hundreds of lessons, without charging me.

I organized a group to purchase the Toney Penna Company in 1988 and to have Toney re-engaged, though he was eighty. But it had side effects. The movie *Other People's Money*, starring Danny DeVito came out a few years later. DeVito played Lenny the Liquidator, a venture capitalist who would break up companies and sell the assets. "The fastest way to go broke is by taking an increasing share in a declining market," DeVito said in the movie.

I soon realized that my first move in my new business life was purchasing a persimmon wood company at a time that metal woods were obsoleting persimmon. The timing could not have been worse.

Penna, who won four PGA Tour events, had a big personality and a short temper. Three weeks into my freshman year at Miami, we went up to play the new Hills course at the Jupiter Hills Club in Tequesta, Florida. I shot a 70 from the back tees with Ken Venturi and the course designer George Fazio watching me. George said, "This guy will attract a bunch of well-to-do members. We'll make him an honorary member here."

That weekend was the official opening of the Village Course. Venturi served as host. Tom Weiskopf and Tommy Bolt, among other prominent golfers, were there. When I arrived I parked my brown and orange Chevy van right in front of the clubhouse. Fazio was fuming for much of the day, wondering whose unsightly van that was. Finally, he learned that it was mine. We were out in the middle of the course by then, and Fazio came out and said to Toney, "Tell that kid of yours to park his van in the staff lot. He will ruin our membership drive."

And Toney, only a few days after Fazio was ready to offer me an honorary membership, shot back, "We don't need your bullshit course anyway," and we left. Ten years later, I became a dues-paying member.

On the way home from a family trip to Europe in 1976, we were connecting through Chicago O'Hare airport. Dad and I were going for a hot dog when he spotted his co-star from the movie *White Christmas*, Danny Kaye. We went over to say hi.

"Didn't you get a group and buy a new baseball team?" Dad said.

"Why yes we bought the new franchise, the Seattle Mariners. You still have a piece of the Pirates, don't you Bing?"

"Yes, Danny, been with them for a long time. Say. What league are the Mariners going into?"

"The American League," Kaye said.

"The American League? Don't they pitch underhand in the American League?" Dad replied.

Flash forward nine years. I was backstage at an event at Cypress Gardens Resort in Orlando, Florida, with other athletes, notably Bob Griese, the Dolphins quarterback, Ted Williams, and Yankees owner George Steinbrenner. We were there receiving awards; mine was for Florida Amateur Athlete of the year, based on my Amateur victory.

Steinbrenner was getting front-page headlines virtually every day, for getting into verbal spats with his players, among them Reggie Jackson, whose ego was of a similar size to Steinbrenner's.

"Nathaniel, I am a great friend of your instructor Toney Penna," he said to me. "We are so proud of you for winning the U.S. Amateur. We wished that your dad was here to see it, but I know that he would be proud, too. If you're ever in New York, please call me and you can watch some Yankee games in my box. It would be a thrill for me to host you."

My response was spontaneous, without a filter, as though the O'Hare/Danny Kaye meeting had happened the day before.

"Mr. Steinbrenner, the Yankees are in the American League, right? Don't they pitch underhand in the American League?"

For a kid of twenty, it might have come off cocky and Mr. Steinbrenner glared at me, as if to say, "Are you kidding?" But there is no denying that one will imitate his parent.

THE CAST OF CHARACTERS THAT ENRICHED DAD'S LIFE, and ours, was long, but perhaps no one better fit the definition of a character than Phil Harris. Harris was a multitalented entertainer—a singer and songwriter, a comedian, an actor, an orchestra leader, and, most notably, a voiceover in renowned animated films, including Disney's *The Jungle Book* and *The Aristocats*. His was the voice for Baloo in *The Jungle Book*, singing the hit *Bear Necessities*.

He also was an avid golfer and outdoorsman, which endeared him to my father. They frequently appeared together in *The American Sportsman* series on television, hosted by renowned sports broadcaster Curt Gowdy. In 2001, Gowdy recounted for ESPN their participation in the series, noting that at any moment in the middle of a hunt an act was likely to break out:

"Oh, Mister Crosby?"

"Is that you, Mister Harris?"

"Indeed it is, Mister Crosby, and how is your day going?"

"Poorly, Mister Harris."

"Oh really, and why is that, Mister Crosby?"

"I forgot my socks, Mister Harris, and my feet are turning blue."

The camera then showed Dad's boots and his bare ankles, whereupon a chuckling Mister Harris would offer Mister Crosby something liquid to warm his toes.

Something liquid was another Harris feature; he was a prolific drinker, who made famous the line, "If I knew that I was going to live this long, I would have taken better care of myself."

He also once said, ominously, in hindsight, "You know, it's proven that you can get just as drunk on water." He paused for effect, then added, "As you can on land."

My brother Harry was fishing with Phil off the shore from our home in Las Cruces, Baja California, when a sudden and severe squall came up and capsized their boat about 400 yards from shore. Phil was seventy at the time and well into the bourbon that afternoon and told Harry to swim to shore and save himself. Harry, fifteen and exceptionally strong for his age, ignored Harris's command and put the 220-pound man we called Uncle Phil on his back. Harris, meanwhile, had passed out.

Harry with Harris in tow made it to shore, but in a desolate area about four miles from civilization. Harry dragged him far enough from the water to avoid incoming waves and performed CPR on him until he began coughing up saltwater. Then Harry ran four miles to seek help, but when they returned, Harris was missing, the sun had set, and the concern was that the incoming tide might have swept him out to sea. Ninety minutes later, Dad, hotel guests, and maybe twenty *marineros*, all equipped with flashlights, found Phil sitting Indian style on a knoll.

Phil did not remember a thing. But score an assist for brother Harry, who allowed us to enjoy another of my father's friend for an extra twenty-five years.

The night that Dad died, Phil was a guest on *Monday Night Football.* He was asked about the news of Dad's death.

"Taking Bing Crosby from us," he said, "was God's first mistake."

# CHAPTER 9

# CROSBY AND HOPE:
# ROAD TO THE GOLF COURSE

Bob Hope and my father were inextricably linked by the seven *Road* films they made together and by the golf they played together. One can only imagine what my father's rounds of golf with Hope were like—probably much like this, as Dad wrote regarding their arrival at the Wentworth Club in England one day in 1961:

> We drove up to the caddie house in our rented Bentley, and Hope immediately asked the caddie master for the best caddie in the place.
>
> "I have just the lad for you," said the caddie master. "Hawkins here is Class A." Hawkins came forth and Hope proceeded to interrogate him.
>
> "Do you know the distances here?" Hope queried.
>
> "I do, sir," the caddie replied.

"Are you familiar with all the bunkers, their depth and their placement?"

"Aye, sir," replied the caddie.

"Are you familiar with the speed of the greens?"

"I am, indeed, sir."

"M-m-m," said Hope. "How are you at finding balls in the heather?"

"Oh, very good, sir," was the caddie's reply.

Hope nodded happily, and then said, "Well, find one, and we'll start."

The rounds of golf my father and Hope played with one another over the years numbered in the hundreds, and each of them surely played out with nonstop banter and money exchanging hands in the end. "He never stopped talking during the eighteen holes," Dad said. "Always doing routines, trying out gags on his playing companions that he could use later on the radio to see how they played. You know. Testing the material." Hope said that Dad hated to lose and when he did, he'd push for a double-or-nothing bet covering an additional three holes, numbers ten through twelve at Lakeside Golf Club, what they used to call the Oregon Short Line and call the Whiskey Route now.

There is a scene in the film *Variety Girls* in which they both star as themselves. At one point, my father and a woman are discussing a round of golf he played with Hope at Altoona on behalf of the Red Cross.

"That's the only time that creaky comic ever beat me," Dad says in the film.

Later, Dad wrote a story on Hope for a magazine called *Professional Golfer* and recalled that scene: "Bob bribed the scriptwriters to put those lines in the picture," he wrote. "It's the only way he has been able to win a game from me."

Dad and Hope arguably were the two most significant entertainment personalities of the twentieth century, yet they were never rivals, even as they were sometimes portrayed as such. They were dear friends, except on the golf course, where they were quite competitive.

They first met outside the Friars Club in New York City in October 1932. A few weeks later, in the waning days of vaudeville, they were working together at the Capitol Theatre—Hope the master of ceremonies and comedian, Dad the singer. They were doing as many as three shows a day, and during their breaks they hurried over to a driving range owned by a prominent teaching pro, Alex Morrison, beneath the 59th Street Bridge. Together, they hit balls until it was time to return to the theater, meanwhile establishing a bond that remained intact the rest of their lives.

Dad already was a member at Lakeside Golf Club in Toluca Lake, California, near several movie studios. He later joined Wilshire and Bel-Air country clubs as well. When Hope moved into the neighborhood, Dad invited him to join him at Lakeside. On many mornings before work, they met there and were off the first tee by 6:30 or so, pending wager negotiations. They played nine holes or more, and were on the set by 9:00. Dad was a better player than Hope, who was a better negotiator on the first tee. "He was always thirty minutes arranging a match," Dad had said. "In the meantime, a crowd would collect and then he'd do a monologue. He would wiggle around, you know, all kinds of plays—induce you to make a match you couldn't win."

THEY PLAYED INNUMERABLE ROUNDS DURING THE WAR, ALL of them raising money on behalf of the war effort. "Over a period stretching from 1941 through 1945 Hope and I played for the Red Cross, for other wartime charities, and for bond drives," my father wrote in his book *Call Me Lucky*. "When we played for bond drives we held a bond sale on the eighteenth green at the conclusion of our match. Our articles of golf apparel, the balls we'd played with, our clubs, anything we had in our baggage, were auctioned off and the money went for bonds. We played in so many cities and on so many courses that I lost count of them."

At Dad's tournament in Rancho Santa Fe, California, in February of 1942, he and Hope were having lunch with PGA president Ed Dudley and tournament bureau manager Fred Corcoran, who asked if they'd be amenable to playing a series of exhibition matches under the PGA banner starting with the Tour's Texas swing. The idea was that the names Crosby and Hope, teaming with PGA stars, would help transcend golf and allow for greater interest and more money raised. They readily agreed. This officially marked the beginning of their wartime golf contributions, and the dawning of a new golf audience.

Their first match, at Brook Hollow Golf Club in Dallas, also featured Ben Hogan and Byron Nelson, among others, and was called "Dallas' most glamorous golf show of all time," by *The Dallas Morning News*. It delivered the largest gallery

in Dallas golf history, too, with an estimated 7,000 in attendance. The next day, they were in Houston and drew 10,000,
the largest crowd in Texas golf history, exceeding even that of
the U.S. Open the previous year at Colonial Country Club in
Fort Worth. More importantly, they raised $30,000 for the war
effort.

Both played in the Texas Open in San Antonio in an effort
to boost the gate and raise money for the American Women's
Voluntary Services. They were paired in the first round with
Ben Hogan and Byron Nelson, ensuring a huge crowd.

On the fifth hole, Dad was in the fairway pondering the distance to the pin. "What do I need to get home?" he asked his
caddie.

"Mr. Crosby," the caddy replied, "I don't even know where
you live."

Dad was certain that Hope was writing the caddy's material.

They played exhibitions with a variety of celebrities, including Babe Didrikson Zaharias, one of the greatest female
athletes in history. Babe won two gold medals in the 1932
Olympic Games in Los Angeles, one in the javelin. Dad had
asked her about the javelin gold medal, about what was going
through her head as she was making the toss. She explained to
him that she was supposed to have had a date with a Norwe-
gian sprinter, who had stood her up. "I pretended I was throwing the javelin right through the middle of his heart," she had
told Dad.

Among the many fundraisers was one that included another Babe, Babe Ruth, as well as California Governor Culbert
Olson, at Haggin Oaks Golf Course in Sacramento, Califor-

nia. Here's how my father recalled the occasion in an interview many years later with *Newsday*'s Joe Gergen:

> We were taking the train—it was The Lark, a very famous and elegant train in those days, from Glendale up the Coast. Babe's wife came to the station with him and took us aside. She told us Babe hadn't been feeling well, that he went to bed early and we shouldn't expect him to engage in any social activity. We said, fine, we'd look out for him.
>
> That night we drifted into the club car and soon Babe had a bottle of bourbon and some cigars. At midnight we went to bed and Babe was still there. At one, I got up to check and Babe was still there. At seven, he knocked on the door and wanted to know the day's schedule. His head hadn't hit the pillow. We got to Sacramento, had breakfast with the governor and then played a round of golf. Babe had never changed clothes.

Hope said, "It was the morning after for the Babe. He hit left-handed and the crowd couldn't get used to his slice. It looked like the Normandy landings. He hit eight people. You could have made a fortune selling Band-Aids." Hope and Ruth, however, still prevailed over Dad and the governor, one-up. An estimated 10,000 spectators showed up, each paying twenty-five cents, with all proceeds going to the Red Cross. Afterwards, Hope and my father went to Mather and McClellan Army Air Base and entertained the enlisted men there.

This was not an atypical day. My father and Hope reportedly played thirty-five exhibition matches that first year alone, generating tremendous proceeds in donations and war bonds, and they often entertained troops afterwards. A renowned columnist for the *Hearst* newspaper chain, Bob Considine, was among the first to note their selflessness: "The best part about the Crosby and Hope exhibitions is that they are wholly unselfish. Those guys need publicity about as much as they need a hole in the head. They pay their own way, sell defense bonds on the side and put on shows at night at the nearest Army camps. In addition they can play in the 70s."

Dad was asked in an interview once what the least and most he had been paid for singing. "I've worked all night for three bucks and played the drums, too, when the band was playing college proms at the University of Gonzaga. On the other hand, one song brought me $50,000 when a gentleman on the Oakland golf course paid that much for a war bond in exchange for hearing me warble."

THE YEAR 1944 WAS A PERSONALLY FULFILLING ONE FOR my father, who won an Academy Award for best actor for his portrayal of Father O'Malley in the film *Going My Way*, had six number-one records, and one of the top-rated radio shows. But it had to have been bittersweet and exhausting, too. The war continued, and, as such, so did the fundraising and entertaining troops.

On July 4th, 1944, Hope and my father played an exhibition at the Los Angeles Country Club, each of them pairing with a top amateur. A *United Press International* story reported that $800,000 in war bonds were sold, while a post-round auction brought in another $200,000. That night, Dad served as the master of ceremonies at the Military Musical Spectacle at the Hollywood Bowl, drawing a crowd of 20,000.

Both are in the World Golf Hall of Fame, for their multiple contributions to the game, including their promoting it and their tireless efforts using the game to help the war effort. Both were actively involved with the United Service Organization (USO) during the war and Hope did fifty-seven USO tours over a fifty-year period. U.S. and world leaders and the military understood what their contributions to the war effort meant. Presidents, generals, kings and queens, and other leaders of the allied nations had a bond with Hope and my father, all having contributed in their own ways to world events that might have turned out differently had they not all been engaged.

My father, like so many others who similarly contributed to the war effort, never would have called himself a hero. But for a proud son at a safe remove from history it is how I often think of him. Those of his standing don't usually have a surfeit of time, but whenever a worthy cause came calling he made himself available. He was as selfless a man as I've ever known.

I DID NOT KNOW BOB HOPE WELL UNTIL AFTER MY FATHER'S death. In 1980, Bob invited me to play with him in the Bob Hope Chrysler Classic. Our third amateur was former president Gerald Ford, and our professional in the first round at Indian Wells Country Club was defending champion John Mahaffey. We were playing our ninth hole when play was halted because of rain. We were escorted to the clubhouse and into the general manager's office to wait out the weather.

What ensued was in essence an hour-long interview, Hope asking the questions and President Ford answering them. It was a veritable tutorial on Middle East issues and the oil crisis that had resulted in gas rationing. My thought was that Roger Mudd, Dan Rather, or Walter Cronkite could not have moderated the discussion any better. Hope's questions were astute and pointed. Mahaffey and I just sat there mesmerized, absorbing a seminar on foreign affairs. Too bad I could not have received high school credit for the event, but it gave me a lifelong memory. I was able to play with Bob and President Ford multiple times at the Hope and at The Jackie Gleason Inverarry Classic.

IN 1989, HOPE, EIGHTY-SIX, WAS HEADING TO ASIA, WHERE he was scheduled to perform eight shows in eleven days in five cities in five different countries: Tokyo, Kuala Lumpur, Hong Kong, Taipei, and Jakarta. Toney Penna, from whom I bought the equipment company, went to Hope and suggested he take me with him, since it might allow me to establish some Asian accounts.

"How do I convince him to come?" Hope asked Penna.

"Why don't you give him ten grand?" Penna said in his usual blunt style. "He's twenty-seven years old and he could use the extra dough." So Hope made the offer and I accepted.

On the day of departure, I went to Hope's estate in Toluca Lake, California, for the limousine ride to the airport. He took took me upstairs and cut me a check for $10,000. For a twenty-seven-year-old earning an annual salary of maybe $40,000 at Penna Golf, that was a substantial sum. He then asked whether I thought it would be a good idea to bring along some golf clubs to auction off after the shows.

"Why not?" I replied.

So my then-wife and I joined him and his wife, Dolores, another couple, friends of the Hopes, and the Hopes' assistant on this trip. We never touched our luggage the entire time. We flew first class, the only fourteen-hour flight I've ever taken where I was disappointed that it ended. It was like lounging in a living room with a team of flight attendants and a call button. We stayed in the finest hotels.

It was an amazing trip with a remarkable man. Throughout meals, Bob would entertain us, riffing jokes, basically testing material. Whatever we laughed at became part of his routine that night. We were his focus group.

Every afternoon was spent on the golf course, Hope and I playing nine holes. I recall that he whistled when he played, on every swing. He was still sneaky good even though he was eighty-six years old. After our nine holes, he'd return to the hotel to rest, then would put on a show at night, even incorporating me into his monologues, with coaching beforehand.

In Tokyo, he was performing at a black-tie event in front of an audience of about 12,000. I was included in a short monologue, and once again a Crosby was playing straight man for Hope. He also had condensed the ABC telecast of my U.S. Amateur victory into a five-minute segment that he played for the crowd. I reckon I received more exposure for my Amateur win in those five minutes than when it aired originally on ABC eight years earlier.

Taiwan, meanwhile, was in a boom economy in 1989, and at the show in Taipei, he auctioned an otherwise worthless Lynx Prowler wedge for $250,000 for charity. The next night in Kuala Lumpur, Malaysia, he auctioned an old Acushnet Bulls Eye putter and was disappointed when the high bid came in at $7,500. He rebounded in Tokyo, however, fetching $250,000 for a MacGregor driver. At first Bob didn't understand the uneven market value of one of his old clubs country to country, until I explained to Bob that they loved him just as much in Malaysia as they did in Taiwan, but that there just wasn't the same amount of wealth.

When we returned home, the first thing we did after landing was head to Lakeside Country Club to play nine holes. I was ready to go straight to bed and sleep for three days, but his having traveled a majority of weeks of every year for decades had taught him that this was the best way to acclimate quickly to a change in time zones.

We had had a great time together on this trip. I believe he enjoyed getting to know the son of his old *Road* partner and friend and I certainly enjoyed getting to know him better. The fact that I shared his passion for golf was a bonus. It was the memory of a lifetime to be able to spend almost two weeks with Bob and Dolores, and I got paid.

That trip allowed me to bring to a close an important chapter in the life of my father, as I have been similarly able to do with so many of his friends, my friends, who had played integral roles in Dad's life and eventually my own life, on and off the course.

After Hope died, in 2003, a wonderful postscript arrived via e-mail, reaffirming this. It was from Kevin Carter, a teaching professional at Medina Golf & Country Club in Medina, Minnesota:

> *Hello Mr. Crosby,*
>
> *In 1981, I was the assistant pro at an exclusive St. Paul club. Mr. Bob Hope came there to play yearly when he was in town. He played at this club because it was always quiet, very few members, and those who were there knew to leave him alone. He happened to be there on the day of the final round of the U.S. Amateur in 1981.*
>
> *It wasn't a nice day, as I recall. Very few members even then would normally be at the club. Mr. Hope went out to play the front 9 alone. It was so quiet that day that I went to the men's grill to watch the final round of the tournament. I'm pretty sure that you remember who was playing.*
>
> *Mr. Hope stopped after 9 holes just as the event came on TV. I nervously jumped up not wanting to bother him. He quietly asked me to sit down. He sat down in the chair right next to me. I was scared to death. He asked me how the tournament was going, I stated that you were tied or one up at that point. Mr. Hope asked me if I would mind watching the tournament with him for a while. I couldn't believe it. It was like watching TV with the nicest Uncle you've ever had. He was so gentlemanly, quiet, and*

*unassuming and every chance that he had, he spoke of you with pride. It was an afternoon I will never forget. He watched the entire tournament without going back out to play by himself.*

*Mr. Crosby, when you won, there were tears streaming down his face. I hope that you know how much he thought of you.*

*Sorry to bother you with such a long e-mail, I just wanted to share this memory with you.*

*Kind Regards,*
*Kevin Carter*
*PGA Teaching Professional*
*Medina Golf and Country Club*

# CHAPTER 10

# THE CROSBY CLAMBAKE

The Bing Crosby National Pro-Am was at one time the most popular tournament on the PGA Tour, more so than even the major championships; in 1971, it was the top-rated golf tournament in television history to that point. It is still played today, though now under the AT&T Pebble Beach National Pro-Am banner, and still is exceedingly popular. Dad pioneered the pro-am, which has been a boon to charities around the country and the world. "It's hard to imagine a regular tour event today without the pro-am," columnist Jim Murray once wrote. "Corporate America embraced the idea like a lovesick octopus." I believe he would be thrilled that the tournament has survived him, with its format intact—four rounds on three courses, with amateur participation in all four rounds and money raised for charity.

Every PGA Tour event other than the Players Championship features a pro-am that financially supports local charities and allows their corporate sponsors to entertain clients. The PGA Tour boasts that it has contributed upwards of $2,000,000,000 to charities through the years. And it began with the Bing Crosby Pro-Am.

"The biggest kick I get out of the tournament is the charities it serves," Dad wrote in a letter. "It always seems a wonderful thing to me that any event, which affords so much pleasure to so many people, players, and spectators alike, can at the same time be developing funds for worthwhile causes . . . pretty painless way of doing a public service, it seems to me."

In 1934, Dad had bought a sixty-five-acre ranch with an adobe house in old Rancho Santa Fe, California, just north of San Diego. The Rancho Santa Fe Country Club, a course designed by Max Behr, a disciple of renowned course architect Alister MacKenzie, was nearby. Dad loved the golf course and the area, the latter to an extent that he became a founder of the Del Mar Race Track, "where the turf meets the surf," as the song goes, sung by my father and still played at the track there.

"I had a home and racetrack interests there in 1937," he told *The New York Times*. "I was playing a lot of golf then. I thought it would be a good idea to get some of my show business pals and the pros together in a pro-amateur tournament. There weren't any. I knew my friends wanted to get acquainted with the pros and imitate the way they hit the ball. So we started at Rancho Santa Fe and the proceeds went to charity."

Thus, the Bing Crosby Pro-Am was born and held for the first time in February 1937 at Rancho Santa Fe Golf Club. Its debut was inauspicious, the weather failing to cooperate. Torrential rain made the roads to the golf course impassable on the day the first of two rounds was scheduled. My father drove up to the Carlsbad hotel where the players were staying and met with Fred Corcoran, the PGA tournament manager. "Fred, the bridges are washed out. I know you boys have a long hop to Houston ahead of you. Here's the check for the full purse, $3,000. Do what you think is fair."

Corcoran, to his credit, said they would play to the contract, weather permitting. The rain finally stopped that night and the tournament, reduced to a single round, was played the following day and was won by Sam Snead, who was presented with a check for $500. "If it's all the same to you, Mr. Crosby, I'd rather have cash," Snead purportedly said, this coming from a man whose legend was partly a work of fiction, including the story passed down through the years that he kept his money in cans buried in his yard.

After the golf was finished, Dad hosted a party for the participants at his house. "A pretty good little soiree," he wrote, "lasting far into the night and necessitating the aid of the highway patrol to guide some of the more bibulous participants to their pads in Del Mar, La Jolla, Oceanside, and San Clemente." The tournament's identity was forged from the beginning by Crosby weather, and, to this day, inclement weather is still called "a pretty good little soiree," which set a tone that still exists and resulted in the event's unofficial title, the Crosby Clambake, that suggests revelry.

The Crosby Clambake was played in Rancho Santa Fe through 1942, when World War II intervened. After the war, Dad sold his house in Rancho Santa Fe and his interest in the

Del Mar Race Track, and had a house built adjacent to the thirteenth fairway at Pebble Beach Golf Links. He also was a member of the Cypress Point Club in Pebble Beach. The Monterey Peninsula, meanwhile, was in the throes of a struggling economy. Ted Durein, the sports editor of the *Monterey Herald*, was part of a group brainstorming ways to boost the economy in the area. Someone came up with the idea of a golf tournament, so Durein set out to raise the money required to host a PGA event. He was unable to do so, but he came up with an alternate plan and wrote a letter to my father:

> *There is a group of sports-minded persons on the Monterey Peninsula who would like to bring a big-time tournament here. We wondered if you would be open to a suggestion to hold it on one of our courses.*

Dad embraced the idea. "To be allowed to stage a golf tournament in such environs is like the *Louvre* granting choice gallery space to an aspiring artist so he can display his efforts," he said on one occasion. On another, he said, "Pebble Beach is the *Louvre*. It just isn't the *Louvre*, it's everything in the *Louvre*, too, with all the artists gathered around."

His first call was to Fred Corcoran. "Fred, is there any reason we can't move the tournament to Pebble Beach and play it over the three peninsula courses?" he asked, speaking of Pebble Beach Golf Links, Cypress Point Club, and Monterey Peninsula Country Club. The only possible reason they couldn't was that Joe Novak, the president of the PGA, thought it should be contested on one course. Dad fortunately prevailed.

Meanwhile, he offered to foot the $5,000 bill himself. When the PGA increased its required minimum to $10,000, Dad did not flinch; he wrote the check.

It quickly became one of the most important tournaments in the history of the game. "It is impossible to measure the worth of the Crosby to golf," Jim Murray wrote. "It changed the format of every tournament ever played. A pro-am became an integral part of nearly every tour stop played."

Celebrities gave the Crosby the cachet it still enjoys. Bill Murray is a perennial contestant and the clown prince of the event, though he takes the game seriously and teamed with D.A. Points to win the pro-am in 2011, while Points was winning the tournament itself.

The amateurs, including the celebrities in their ranks, have infused the tournament with color. When stories are told through the years, virtually none have to do with how any particular tournament was won, but how the relationships and partnerships were formed.

One of the most entertaining players in the history of the tournament and the history of the movie business was acclaimed actor Jack Lemmon, whose long quest to make the cut was never realized. He began playing the tournament in 1958 as a result of his having starred in the film *Operation Mad Ball* alongside Kathryn Grant, my mother, who would soon marry my father. When she learned that Lemmon was a golf nut, she had my father extend an invitation to him to play.

"Jack Lemmon can't play at all, but he loves the game. He can't even break 120," Dad told Joe Gergen of *Newsday* years later. "I'll never forget one year he was on the fourteenth tee.

There was a big gallery around and he was very nervous. He stood over the ball, going back and forth, back and forth with the club. Finally, a mongrel dog ran onto the tee, dashed right between his legs, and disappeared into the gallery. Jack just went ahead and swung. I caught up to him three holes later and congratulated him on his remarkable composure. He said, 'You mean that was a real dog?' "

Dad also once said that Lemmon with a golf club in his hands "looks like he's basting a turkey." Another time it was, "Jack looks like a chambermaid sweeping under the bed."

Demon rum played a recurring role at the Crosby. The entertainer Phil Harris, one of Dad's closest friends and a noted tippler, liked to claim he was playing out of Jack Daniels Country Club, and when the weather went south he would identify it as "double-brandy weather." Tour pro Lawson Little had a home in nearby Monterey that was called Gibson Gulch as a result of his skill in mixing the martinis that kept his guests refreshed throughout tournament week. "He prepares weeks before the tournament for the influx of visitors and fills his basement with gallon jugs of martinis," Dad wrote. "He goes down once a day and gives the jugs a half turn just so they don't settle too much. There's little doubt but that he gets his associates in such physical condition he could win the tournament easy if he could just refrain from participating in his own hospitality."

Francis Brown was an accomplished amateur golfer and wealthy Hawaiian who owned the land on which the Mauna Lani Resort on the Big Island was built. Brown was a frequent participant in the Crosby and was among those who enjoyed a libation (or few!) at night. On one particular occasion, the professional with whom he was partnered took exception to Brown's condition, which my father would have described as having the "whips and jingles," the term he used for hangover-induced shakes. His professional partner was concerned that Brown's condition would preclude him from playing well and possibly costing him money.

"What's first prize for you in the pro-amateur division?" Brown asked his professional partner.

"A thousand dollars," the pro replied, at which point Brown removed his money clip and peeled off ten $100 bills.

"OK, here's the thousand," Brown said. "Now let's play golf."

Dad was not immune to the revelry, either. Brown held an annual "do," as he called it, at his home atop a hill in the Del Monte Forest. He was with Lindsay, one of his sons from his first marriage, who was thirteen at the time. My father initially declined the invitation to go to Brown's party because he had Lindsay with him, but Brown convinced him to bring him along, too.

"But the night wore on beyond what had been my original intention, and the first thing I knew we were coming down the hill and it was four a.m.," Dad wrote in the prologue to the book *The Crosby: The Greatest Show in Golf.* "The back seat was full of revelers, and Linny was in the front seat with me. We made it all right. The next day Linny was gallerying Bob Hope's foursome, and Bob came over and said, 'How did you get home last night?' Linny said, 'We made it all right.' And Bob said, 'Well, you didn't let your father drive in the condition he was in.' Linny thought for a moment and then said, 'He was the best we had.' "

\* \* \*

ONE YEAR, PHIL HARRIS HOLED WHAT WAS DESCRIBED AS A ninety-foot putt with a huge break on the seventeenth hole. Was it really ninety feet, he was asked? "Hell, it broke that much," he replied. At any rate, it sealed a victory for him and his professional partner Dutch Harrison. "How about that, Bing?" Harris said. "Ain't this a helluva blow to clean living?"

Harris was a character, who was likely to say anything at any time, without regard to being politically correct. On the telecast once he was asked whether he knew PGA Tour player Gay Brewer. "Gay Brewer?" he said. "I thought he was a fag winemaker from Modesto."

Some professionals complained that the wind was so strong they couldn't keep their golf ball on the tee. Peter Hay, the professional at Pebble Beach and a proper Scot accustomed to golf in the worst conditions, was aghast. "Why, there's no rule in the book that says you have to put it on the tee," he said.

Jim Murray called the tournament "the road to pneumonia." Johnny Weissmuller, the actor best known for his starring role in six Tarzan films, also had been an Olympic swimmer who won five gold medals. After exiting the course after playing in a steady downpour in the Bing Crosby Pro-Am one year, he said, "I've never been so wet in my life."

The weather was also miserable in 1967, forcing delays. Finally, with the tournament nearing completion, Billy Casper leading, and Arnold Palmer and Jack Nicklaus tied for second, Palmer hit a prodigious drive at the par-five fourteenth hole. He took a three-wood for his second shot, and the ball on its descent clipped a branch of a pine tree and caromed out of bounds. He took a drop and hit another three-wood that clipped the same tree and went out of bounds again. He took a nine on the hole and eventually finished third.

The weather got revenge on Palmer's behalf, though. Overnight, the storm returned and uprooted the tree.

My father generally took a pragmatic view of the weather. "Maybe that's part of the character of the area and the tournament that makes it unique," he said. "Nobody asks me who won the event. It's always, 'How was the weather?' "

There was discussion from time to time of shifting the tournament to a date later in the year to improve the likelihood of better weather. On one such occasion, Dad, in a letter to Joe Dey, the commissioner of the PGA Tour, wrote that their research showed the weather was not appreciably better in March, but that competition from televised events from other sports was greater that time of year. So it continued to be held in winter, weather notwithstanding.

The likelihood of miserable weather was never a deterrent to amateurs seeking invitations to play—the invitation itself is a keepsake for many. Glenn Frey, a singer and guitarist with the Eagles, said, "It's not like any other piece of mail you get." That is, the weather never prevented these amateurs and pros alike from getting their coveted invitations.

One story, entirely possible too, involved a man on the East Coast in the midst of marital problems while he awaited his invitation to play in the Crosby. During one particular argument, his wife confessed to having received his invitation and tossing it in the fireplace. The man immediately phoned his lawyer and instructed him to prepare to file for divorce.

Dad gave serious thought to whom to extend invitations, given their limited number and the thousands who wanted to play in his tournament. "Some of the requests are classic," Dad told *Golf Digest*. "One year a man wrote me saying he had survived two heart attacks and he wanted to play in my tournament just once before the fatal one. I put him in, but added a footnote in my letter saying a man with his heart condition really shouldn't be playing those tough courses."

A man once approached tournament director Maurie Luxford, claimed he was holding $25,000, and offered it to him in exchange for an invitation to the tournament. "I'm sorry, but we don't operate that way," Luxford replied. On another occasion, an automobile was offered as a bribe.

My father personally extended an invitation to former president Dwight Eisenhower, a golf nut, to come out and play:

*Dear General Eisenhower:*

*Sam Morse of the Del Monte Properties, Pebble Beach, has told me he has written to you, in the hope that he could entice you westward for our annual Pro-Amateur Golf Tournament at Pebble Beach in late January.*

*All of us would be tremendously happy if you could adjust your schedule, allowing your presence there at that time—either as a player, or as a spectator. I think that you would find it a very enjoyable occasion, and see some fine golf.*

*I would appreciate it if you would let me know whether or not you will be able to come. I am currently in England making a film but plan to be home early in November.*

*Incidentally, we're staying at the home of Dr. Berns and from some of the pictures around the house, it seems likely that you may have been a guest at one time or another when you were here during the war. Happily, the house is located right near Sunningdale, Wentworth, and the Berkshire golf clubs, so we are very conveniently installed.*

*The weather, too, has been unusually kind for England, and we're having some fine games over the weekends. I think sone of these courses are among the greatest in the world.*

*Anticipating a reply from you soon, and with my kindest respects*

*Sincerely yours,*

*Bing*

A week later, the president responded:

*Dear Bing:*

*My golf is entirely too erratic for me even to dream of accepting your kind invitation to participate in the Pebble Beach tournament. This I must say in spite of the fact that Arnold Palmer, whose broad back ought to be able to carry any dub anywhere, expressed a great desire through Maurie Luxford to take me on as a partner. However, I hope to be in Palm Springs in January, and harbor a faint hope that I might be able to run over for one day to see your tournament, about which I have heard so many complimentary things. After my schedule firms up, I will send you an indication as to whether I can make it.*

*I am interested in the fact that you are staying in Mr. Berns' house near Sunningdale. He was very helpful to me, surgically, in 1942. One sunny day I recall that a group of us gathered on his lawn for an outdoor tea or a kind of picnic. Should you happen to see him personally I would be highly pleased if you would convey to him my warm greetings. Thanks again for your nice invitation, and with best wishes to yourself,*

*Sincerely,*

*Dwight D. Eisenhower*

One president who did accept Dad's invitation was Gerald Ford, who on the evening of Jimmy Carter's inauguration in 1977 flew out to Monterey and the next day was playing alongside partner Arnold Palmer in the Crosby at Monterey Peninsula Country Club. A huge crowd turned out. "Where were all these people on election day?" Ford asked jokingly. For Saturday's round there was the largest gallery in tournament history at the time, an estimated 25,000. If they'd all voted for Ford, a tournament official said to him, he would have won the election.

"Yes," he replied. "But then I wouldn't be here."

After the Pittsburgh Pirates won the World Series in 1960, my father, a part owner of the team, invited shortstop Dick Groat, the National League's Most Valuable Player, to play in the Crosby in 1961. He then paired him with Arnold Palmer, the reigning PGA player of the year. "I had won the MVP and Arnold won Golfer of the Year on the PGA Tour, so Bing thought it would be a great pairing," Groat told the *Beaver County Times*. "Arnold was on top of his game and I hadn't been playing golf for very long and I wasn't that great. It was intimidating for me. It was a horrible experience."

Those in the gallery tended to ignore both Palmer and Groat and went straight for my father in pursuit of an autograph. "We were there four days for the tournament, and Bing ruled the roost," Groat said.

The legendary sportswriter Grantland Rice was among the earliest to recognize how important the Crosby had come to be in so short a time:

> If some strong pair of hands should reach out and take a wayfarer by the throat, asking him to name the top all-around golf tournament of the year, there could be only one answer.
>
> A tournament put on by a fellow who sings a little, acts a little, and also plays golf. In fact, he has been named the country's leading all-around entertainer for the last five years. The name is Bing Crosby.
>
> I can tell you why the Crosby tournament . . . is the best of them all including the U.S. Open.
>
> Other tournaments offer prizes from $10,000 to $15,000. So does Bing. Other tournaments charge admission and so pay all the bills, with a nice profit on the side. Bing charges admission and then gives all the receipts to charity.
>
> It costs Bing from $12,000 to $18,000 to put on one

of his shows. Hard-pressed charity gets the big check, minus the prize money.

There's another reason. The U.S. Open, the Los Angeles Open, the Masters and other big tests are held over some fine golf courses. The Bing Crosby tournament is held over three great golf courses—three of the greatest in golf—Pebble Beach, Cypress Point, and Monterey Peninsula.

"Most people in golf have no idea how immensely significant the Crosby format has been in making tournament golf big business," golf writer Herb Graffis said. "Bing came along at the right time with the right idea. When he got that Youth Fund as beneficiary, he caught charity lightning in a bottle."

Television helped elevate the Crosby to the status it continues to enjoy today. People enjoy watching celebrities, even those playing bad golf. My father expressed his love and appreciation for what the Crosby meant to him and the game in his prologue: "Here's the game I've played and loved for forty-five years, being played in the most beautiful environment imaginable on three world-famous links, by the best professionals, amateurs, sportsmen, and friends, and all for the substantial benefit of the most estimable charitable causes. When I think I've had a hand in all this, my cup runneth over."

For all that he accomplished in life, the tournament was what he most wanted to be remembered for. "If I were asked what single thing has given me the most gratification in my long and sometimes pedestrian career," he said, "I think I would have to say it is this tournament."

Some one-on-one time with Dad. (Harry Benson/Getty Images)

On the way to another Pirates game. (Author's personal collection)

Dad entertaining troops during World War II. Some much-needed melody. (Ullstein Bild/Getty Images)

Reading the *Racing Form* at Aqueduct Racetrack, circa 1975. (*New York Daily News* Archive/Getty Images)

Look at those faces. An awkward (and priceless) Christmas show moment.
(Author's personal collection)

Surviving Crosby weather.
(Julian P. Graham/Loon Hill Studio)

My godfather, Jackie Burke,
and Dad, 1963.
(Julian P. Graham/Loon Hill Studio)

Dad with hunting buddy Phil Harris and their canine pal, 1952.
(Julian P. Graham/Loon Hill Studio)

Two pals goofing on the Road to the Links. Bing Crosby and Bob Hope, circa 1951. (Julian P. Graham/Loon Hill Studio)

Phil Harris, James Garner, and Arnold Palmer, 1962 Crosby Pro-Am. (Julian P. Graham/ Loon Hill Studio)

Playing in his last Crosby Pro-Am with partner Ben Hogan, 1956. (Underwood Archives/ Getty Images)

Winning for Dad.
(Author's personal collection)

All-American dinner with Bob Hope and Mom, 1982.
(Ron Galella/Getty Images)

The man himself, presiding over the green. (Julian P. Graham/ Loon Hill Studios)

# CHAPTER 11

# PIRATES, PUGILISTS, HORSES, AND HUNTING

Generally, sports formed the centerpiece of my father's life. The singing and acting? They paid for this entertainer's entertainment, which after golf included, in no order, baseball, horse racing, boxing, hunting, fishing, football, hockey, and tennis. *Even* hockey and tennis.

On the hockey front, he was a shareholder in the Seals, a National Hockey League expansion team in the sixties. The partnership included brothers Mickey and Barry Van Gerbig, the latter known as the Baron and the man who succeeded George Coleman as the president of Seminole. The brothers owned 50 percent of the team, and a large group that included Dad and Coleman owned the other half.

It was expensive running an NHL expansion franchise and the team frequently was running out of money. So the Van Gerbigs and team president Bill Torrey, another of Dad's friends and the man responsible for assembling the New York Islanders' four Stanley Cup champions, put together a capital call at the Top of the Mark at the renowned Mark Hopkins Hotel in San Francisco. Everyone was having a great time, when Dad sidled up next to the piano and sang for a solid two hours. He finally tired and announced that he was heading home, which unexpectedly was a signal to the potential investors that the evening was over. They left before the capital request was made. Compounding that error, the Van Gerbigs and Torrey were left with a $10,000 bill for the evening.

On the tennis front, Dad attended Wimbledon and played at the California Tennis Club in San Francisco. The great *San Francisco Chronicle* gossip columnist Herb Caen recounted an afternoon in 1970 when my father was playing doubles on Court Number One at the California Tennis Club, "hitting every ball on the sweet spot, never double-faulting, always serving to the opponent's backhand and returning everything so his partner could make the eventual putaway." Naturally, as word spread that he was there, a group of about fifty kids gathered to watch. Afterward, a ten-year-old boy asked him to sign four slips of paper.

"What are you going to do, trade these for one Sinatra?" my dad asked jokingly.

"No," the boy replied, without missing a beat, "eight Sinatras."

Dad's interest in sports was rooted in his childhood in Spokane, Washington. "I can remember, in that long twilight up in the Northwest, we played kick the can or duck on the rock or baseball or handball until it finally got dark about 8:30 or 9:00, and our folks would come to get us," he told *Sports Illustrated*. "We lived across the street from a Jesuit college [Gonzaga] in Spokane. The priests encouraged us youngsters to use the baseball diamonds, the handball courts, and the football field. As a kid, I played everything."

This was the arena in which he was most at peace, anything to do with sports and its people.

And this was the life into which I was born. Imagine, a kid in love with sports, whose father shared his passion that came with the additional benefit of unlimited access to games, athletes, clubhouses, even team benches.

At one point, Dad attempted to buy the Boston Braves (now the Atlanta Braves) baseball club, but was rebuffed by the commissioner, Judge Kenesaw Mountain Landis. Judge Landis "hammered his gavel at that point because I was involved in a California racetrack up to my fetlocks—and the judge regarded horse racing as an instrument of the devil," my father wrote. Dad was founder and part owner of the Del Mar Race Track on the coast just north of San Diego. Landis was the baseball commissioner in the wake of the infamous Black Sox scandal and was squeamish about gambling. Dad also was part of a syndicate that bought the Detroit Tigers in 1956, a 7 percent shareholder, but because of his stake in the Pirates, he was forced to sell his Tigers' stock.

The Pittsburgh Pirates had been in the same family since 1900, when it elected to sell the team to a group headed by John Galbreath and Frank McKinney in 1946, for a reported $2.25 million. My father was part of the group, buying a 25 percent interest in the team. He did not meddle in the day-to-day operation of the team, but his ownership stake paid dividends. In 1948, an eighteen-year-old pitcher from Idaho, Vernon Law, was drawing attention from scouts.

I will let Law pick up the story, this from an e-mail exchange I had with him in 2010:

> I'd have to go back to my junior year at Meridian High School. I was playing in a game at Payette, Idaho. At that game was an attorney . . . Herman Welker, who was a friend of Bing. The two of them did a bit of pheasant hunting and fishing together.
>
> I was pitching and was striking out quite a few of their hitters and not letting anyone on base, except for a couple of errors . . . we had a one to nothing lead. They came to bat in [the last inning] and the first hitter comes up and it was their secret weapon, a midget about 3–1/2 feet tall. He of course was up there to get a base on balls. As luck would have it, I threw three straight strikes and struck him out. The other two hitters did the same. So we won 1–0.
>
> This whole event impressed the attorney, Herman Welker, and so being a bird dog, he called his friend, Bing. Because of his interest in the Pirates, Bing called the general manager of the Pirates. They sent out a scout, Babe Herman. I knew nothing about this, as they couldn't talk to any player who had not yet graduated from high school.
>
> When I did graduate on May 20, 1948, I had nine different organizations' scouts there at my house wanting me to sign with their ball clubs. So when each scout came in to talk to my parents . . . they didn't know that we didn't

allow tobacco in the house. Each one had a big cigar in their mouth so my Dad told them, "You can come in but the cigar stays outside." Because of this, they didn't make a real good impression on my folks.

Now when the Pirates came in they had a box of chocolates and a dozen roses for my mom.

Halfway through the presentation, the phone rang. Babe Herman suggested to my mom that she better answer it and to her surprise, Bing was on the other end of the line. My mother, being a great fan of Bing, almost fainted and couldn't believe she was talking to the great Bing Crosby.

In this conversation Bing made some promises to her and said if your son gets to the big leagues and plays in a world series, you'll get an expense paid trip to wherever they play. (And he lived up to that promise as my parents were able to fly back to see the whole series—games in Pittsburgh and in New York.)

He went on to offer some good advice. Don't sign for a bonus. (Back then, if you signed for over $5,000 you had to stay with the Big League Club for two years, not getting a chance to really develop pitching skills). That turned out to be great advice, as I had no idea about a wind-up or what a change-up was or how to set up a hitter. Everything Bing told them made sense and that sealed the deal.

What I didn't know was this was all set up ahead of time and perfectly timed . . . to halfway through the presentation. I didn't know about the cigars until after the Dodgers and Giants moved West. Perhaps you know there were times that Bing would show up at the ballpark and would come to the clubhouse and say, "Hello." It was one visit he made to Dodger Stadium in which I was the starting pitcher, and he asked me if I remembered anything about my signing. And all I knew was who was there and very few particulars. He went on to tell me that the Pirates went out and bought the cigars and then handed them out just before the scouts went in. Herman Welker knew the affect that would have with my parents.

So, yes, Bing was responsible for my signing with the Pirates. During my career I would get a letter offering encouragement as we didn't have a very good club early on . . . I know my record would probably be a lot better had I signed with the Yankees or the Cardinals, even the Dodgers, but I needed to go through . . . those tough times to really appreciate the life changing experience of playing against the best team in baseball, the Yankees, and to beat them in the '60 series.

Again thanks to the greatest singer and man in Hollywood that I had that opportunity.

The Laws were devout Mormons, and Dad knew that Mrs. Law in particular would take offense with smoking. In fact it turned out that Dad had instructed Herman make sure he was the last scout to enter the Law household and only after distributing the cigars to the other scouts, knowing they could not resist smoking them right away. He also instructed Herman to present Mrs. Law with flowers and a box of chocolates and to promise her that Dad would finance their airfare and accommodations to Pittsburgh should the Pirates get to the World

Series. Dad made good on his promise when the Pirates won in 1960 and Vern Law was one of the major stars.

Law won 162 games in sixteen seasons with the Pirates and was awarded the Cy Young Award as the best pitcher in the National League in 1960.

My father went to games whenever he could. In 1948, he and three of his sons from his first marriage went to a spring training game in Los Angeles. They went into the clubhouse before the game, my father with a bag of peanuts in his hands.

"How's things, Kirby?" he said to pitcher Kirby Higbe as he started to eat a peanut. Before he could eat a second peanut, a clubhouse man snatched the bag from my father. "Bad luck eating peanuts in a dressing room," the clubhouse attendant said.

Superstitions are prevalent in baseball, and my father was not immune. "Bing Crosby was always so superstitious," the Pirates shortstop Dick Groat said. "We'd rarely win when he came to the games." When the Pirates won the National League pennant and advanced to the World Series to play the New York Yankees in 1960, Dad was out of the country and opted to stay there. He and my mother had gone to Rome for the Olympic Games, had an audience with Pope John XXIII, and toured parts of Italy and Austria.

"One of the reasons I'm going to Rome is to help the Pirates win," he said before embarking. "Every time I've watched them on TV this year—and that's seven times—they've lost. So I called manager Danny Murtaugh the other day and asked if he thought it would help if I got as far away as Rome. He seemed to think it was worth a try."

They eventually went to Paris and stayed at the home of friends Charles and Nonie de Limur and were there during the World Series. The Series went to a seventh game at Pittsburgh, and Mom and Dad and the de Limurs were listening to it on short-wave radio. The Pirates scored five runs in the bottom of the eighth to take a 9–7 lead and the Yankees tied it in the top of the ninth with two runs. Dad was so nervous he broke open a bottle of Scotch and poured himself a drink. He began nervously tapping the glass against the fireplace mantel. When the Pirates' Bill Mazeroski hit a ninth-inning home run to win the seventh game, Dad, in his excitement, tapped the glass too hard, shattering it and spilling the Scotch into the fireplace, causing a fire that spread to the living room. Mom screamed, but fortunately the fire was quickly extinguished. "It's very nice to celebrate things," Nonie said, "but couldn't we be more restrained?"

That game belongs in any debate about the greatest game ever played, but for fifty years there was no video evidence. Then one day in 2010, Robert Bader, vice president of Bing Crosby Enterprises and former archivist for Major League Baseball, was rummaging around in the basement of our family home in Hillsborough, California, part of a larger effort to locate and preserve Dad's work, when he discovered five gray canisters containing reels of the seventh game. My father, determined to watch the game when he returned to the United States, had hired a company to record the game via kinescope. It was the only known recording, and upon discovery quickly became big news. A side note: The tape was found next to a collection of Dom Perignon that my friends and I might have accessed on prom night or when we began dating a new girl. There were also cases of Olympia beer; my grandfather had been an accountant for Olympia, which was a generous sponsor of my father's tournament for years. Cases were sent to us every year. My friends and I might have sampled those occasionally, too. There was also bootleg whiskey down there, left over from Prohibition. It seems to me that would have made for a better story than a wine cellar.

Nonetheless, the tape was transferred to DVD and aired on the MLB Network and was a huge success. "It was a great film," Groat said. "I will never get tired of watching Game Seven of the 1960 World Series."

A year earlier, I had attended a birthday party for former Major League player Rusty Staub. Frank Cashen, the former general manager of the New York Mets, was there and I saw him talking to Ralph Kiner, a Hall of Famer who had played most of his career with the Pirates and knew my father. Kiner was traded late in his career by the new Pirates' general manager Branch Rickey, who was determined to rid the team of its higher-priced players. I had just read a book called *Roberto* about the life of Roberto Clemente, and it had a story that addressed Rickey and the trade and how angry Kiner had been about it. I introduced myself to Kiner and brought up the book and the trade. He then went off on a tirade that lasted the better part of five minutes. He was still miffed that the Pirates had traded him. "Ralph," I said, "this is great to meet you after all this time, but that was fifty-six years ago. You really need to talk to someone Ralph, you should see a therapist." Kiner took it in good humor. I think.

When a group of the Pirates from the 1960 championship team gathered for a screening of the seventh game at the landmark Byham Theater in downtown Pittsburgh, I repeated the story. Dick Groat was there, as were Bob Friend, Bill Virdon, and Hal Smith, among others, and they laughed hysterically at the fact that Kiner, more than a half century later, could still summon such rage.

At the screening, I was seated next to actor Michael Keaton, or, as we knew him, Batman. A man seated in the next row came over and introduced himself to me.

"I hear you're the biggest Pittsburgh Pirate fan of all time," the man said to me.

"Yeah," I replied. "But I'm afraid that with this MLB revenue-sharing they're doing that they don't have an interest in putting a competitive team on the field." The Pirates were closing in on twenty straight losing seasons.

Unbeknownst to me, the man who had introduced himself was the Pirates' principal owner, Bob Nutting. Fortunately, he was quite gracious about my faux pas and said that they intended to reverse course with the Pirates, as indeed they have.

WHEN MY FATHER FIRST BEGAN TO MAKE MONEY BEYOND what he needed as living expenses he used it to bet on horses. "I made up my mind that if I ever could afford it, I'd own horses of my own," he said. As his wherewithal grew, so did his investments in the business. He bought stock in the new Santa Anita Park a few miles northeast of Los Angeles, "so I could be sure of a box seat on the finish line," he said.

He began buying horses, too, as well as a ranch in Rancho Santa Fe. When he was approached about investing in a racetrack near there, he quickly agreed. He and actor Pat O'Brien financed the track, with my father serving as its first president. Opening day in 1937 resembled a Hollywood movie premiere. Barbara Stanwyck presented the trophy for the feature race, Bette Davis and Robert Taylor were there, and Dad and O'Brien were at the gate to greet the horseplayers as they came through the turnstiles.

"Crosby's presence quickly turned the track into what it is still known as today, "the Saratoga of the West," William Nack wrote in *Sports Illustrated* years later. "For years, Del Mar was a summer haunt for Bing and his friends, a kind of saltwater spa, a place where the Hollywood crowd came to play." Laura Hillenbrand, in her remarkable best-selling book *Seabiscuit*, called it "a magnificent seaside racing palace" and "a Bing paradise, featuring racing by day and dinner, dancing, and crooning by night."

On Saturday nights there, my father would host a party in the Turf Club. "Bing would walk through the clubhouse and invite 150 people, hand pick them," actor Jackie Cooper said. "The minute the last race was over, they'd set up the tables. An orchestra played dance music all night, and Bing would sing."

One of the horses my father owned, High Strike, won the first race at Del Mar, setting him up for a huge letdown, the years of disappointing horses that followed. "The first horse I owned was Zombie, a steed of peerless lineage but dubious ability," he said, which could have described any number of his horses. At a golf outing once, Bob Hope said that my father was supposed to be there, but "one of his horses was dying and Crosby finally wanted to see one of his horses finish."

My father's response was this: "When Hope began to kid me about it on the air, it became legend that my horses were dogs. I played along with this for laughs, since laughs are hard to come by. Hope is always short of good material, and if my horses supplied him with a little radio fodder it was all right with me. My horses cooperated, too."

There were exceptions, two of them notable. One was Ligaroti, owned by my father and Lin Howard, son of Seabiscuit owner Charles Howard. Ligaroti and Seabiscuit ran a match race at Del Mar in 1938 that was billed as father vs. son and Bing. It was heavily promoted and delivered as promised. Years later, Nack in *Sports Illustrated* described it as "one of the damnedest, daringest, hairiest struggles in the history of the American turf.

"The stretch drive was a spectacle. 'They [the jockeys] whipped each other with their whips, grabbed each other's legs, pulled on each other's reins,' says [Sonny] Greenberg. 'I never saw anything like it. Roughest race I ever saw, here or anywhere.'

"Seabiscuit ended up winning it by a nose, to a ringing ovation from the fans, but the stewards were not cheering. In fact, they were furious over the rodeo . . . The stewards suspended both jockeys."

It was "a melee, a Pier Sixer on horseback," my father said, borrowing a renowned wrestling broadcaster's term to describe a free-for-all. He also called it "one of my most treasured memories of Del Mar."

The match race established Del Mar as a bona fide player in the racing business, and it continues to operate seventy-eight years later, with a summer meet and a new Bing Crosby meet in the fall as well as a Kathryn Crosby Stakes and a Bing Crosby Handicap. And the theme song that my father recorded is still played twice a day there—before the first race and after the last race:

*Where the turf meets the surf*
*Down at old Del Mar*
*Take a plane, take a train, take a car.*
*There's a smile on every face*
*And a winner in each race*
*Where the surf meets the turf at*
*Del Mar.*

His other memorable horse was Meadow Court, a British thoroughbred in whom he owned a one-third interest. Meadow Court, ridden by the great English jockey Lester Piggott, won the Irish Derby in 1965 with my father in attendance. He went down to the winner's circle and was quickly surrounded by a throng of racing enthusiasts and Bing Crosby fans. He began singing "When Irish Eyes Are Smiling," though apparently not loud enough for those in the back of the throng to hear him.

"I can't hear you, Bing, I can't hear you," one man shouted in his Irish lilt.

Dad ignored him and kept singing.

"I can't hear you, Bing, I can't hear you," the man said a second time, then a third time. Finally Dad stopped singing.

"Well, what is it that you'd like me to do?" he asked.

"Would you ever stand on your wallet?" the man replied, evoking raucous laughter.

ONE OF MY FATHER'S HORSE RACING CRONIES WAS JOE Frisco, a Vaudevillian who stuttered and had built his fame on jazz dancing, but later become a comedian who incorporated the stuttering into his act. Joe Frisco also was a compulsive gambler. One day at Santa Anita Park, Frisco was there at the Turf Club entrance when my father walked in and he asked my dad for twenty dollars.

"That's quite a large sum, Joe," Dad said. "Why so much this time?"

Frisco said he had received tips from a handicapper with a hot hand, but lacked the means to take advantage.

Dad spotted him the twenty. After several races, news reached my father that Frisco had bet on every winner, had parlayed each of them, and had won six or seven hundred dollars and was in the bar buying drinks for everyone. So my Dad went downstairs to see for himself. En route, he ran into a friend, who confirmed the rumors, only now his winnings were up as high as $1,500.

When Dad got to the grandstand bar, Frisco was there with "thirty or forty admirers," Dad said, in addition to buying drinks, Frisco was shelling out five or ten dollars to friends who weren't having such luck. Dad walked up to Frisco and gave him a stare that suggested he wanted his twenty back.

"Hiya, kid," Frisco said, before continuing to entertain his crowd.

"Joe," Dad said, "how about, er, you know?"

"Here, kid," Frisco said, peeling off a twenty-dollar bill and handing it to Dad. "Sing me a chorus of 'Melancholy Baby.' "

Dad said he was so taken aback that he went ahead and sang the song as requested.

HORSES WEREN'T THE ONLY ANIMALS IN WHICH HE WAS IN-terested. He was an avid outdoorsman who made frequent appearances on the television show *American Sportsman*. There was marlin fishing in Mexico, salmon fishing in the River Derwent in Tasmania, Australia, fly-fishing in Cockermouth, England, hunting sand grouse in the Northern Highlands of Africa. And shows in which Dad appeared were generally the highest rated of the series.

One of Dad's closest friends was Phil Harris, a multitalented entertainer, who often participated in these shows, too. "We had some wonderful guests, but those two were the best," the show's host, the legendary sports broadcaster Curt Gowdy said. "They used to sit up half the night talking about what they'd say to each other and composing songs they'd sing in the field."

My father was a good shot, Gowdy said, but Harris was a great shot, "one of the best I ever saw in my life. Phil was a great wing shot."

One year, they were doing a segment on pheasant hunting in Nebraska. Harris brought along a .410 shotgun with which their host, from the Nebraska Game and Fish Department, took exception.

"You can't kill pheasants with that pop gun," the man said.

"You can," Harris replied without skipping a beat, "if you hit 'em in the head."

Dad enjoyed going on African safaris. He took my mother with him on a couple of occasions. On one such occasion, they took friends Vic and Helen Bergeron along to Kenya. Vic is the man who founded the Trader Vic's restaurant chain that still exists around the world, including Trader Vic's Mai-Tai Lounge at the Beverly Hilton Hotel in Beverly Hills, California. Bergeron also is credited with inventing the Mai-Tai. The Bergerons lived down the street from us and were frequent dinner guests. "All in all it was a wonderful holiday we will never forget," Trader Vic wrote, recalling the safari in a Christmas letter, "and then to add to this pleasure, Bing and Kathy—who are the greatest of kids for making up songs—made up this little ditty about the safari, things around the camp and the whole holiday, and sent me one of the tapes. I thought it would be a grand thing to give away for this Christmas, and so we are giving this to you with our best wishes for a very happy holiday, Sincerely, Trader Vic."

My mother might have been a bona fide golf widow, but she strategically became an avid hunter, which allowed her to accompany Dad on many of his excursions. In addition to their annual African safaris, they hunted geese at Dad's Rising River Ranch in Northern California, ducks on the Sacramento Delta, and quail in Texas, South Carolina, and Georgia, courtesy of many of Dad's close friends who coincidentally had large southern plantations.

Mom may have avoided marriage counseling, which she undoubtedly would have been attending alone, by becoming an accomplished and enthusiastic hunter.

CHAPTER 12

## ON PARENTING

I had a recurring dream after my father died that he was on his deathbed and had said to me, "I love you." I'd always wanted to hear this, but never did as far as I can recall. Maybe in his day it wasn't manly to say it to your children or to your friends. I take the opposite approach and tell each of my kids that I love them with each telephone call or visit. They return the sentiment, unless, of course, I deny a financial request from them.

Dad even had an aversion to the phrase "I love you" in his songs. He famously instructed songwriter Johnny Burke to avoid it. When Burke wrote the lyrics to the song "Moonlight Becomes You," which Dad would sing in the film *Road to Morocco,* he included the caveat "If I say": "If I say I love you I want you to know it's not just because there's moonlight although, moonlight becomes you so." When Dad's instructing his songwriters to avoid requiring him to sing the words, you shouldn't expect too much of that kind of show of affection on the home front.

"My slant on buttering up is this: There's an old Italian proverb that says never kiss a baby unless he's asleep," my father wrote in his book *Call Me Lucky*. "This should apply not only to babies but to teenagers, until they've reached an age where their judgment tells whether the 'you're so wonderful' line tossed in their direction is flattery or not. Even if it's not I don't think that kids can handle that kind of praise. When I want to be especially flattering to one of my offspring I say, 'nice going' and let it go at that."

Years later, he told our butler, Alan Fisher, "If you keep telling these kids how great they are they are going to start believing it, and that may not be a good thing."

He was less reserved talking about us with others. In a letter to Ben Hogan, dated April 15, 1977, he wrote, "My two boys are playing well. Nathaniel particularly. He's the keenest about the game. Just won a tournament over in Oakland—a Junior Tournament—and if the amount of time he puts into it and the zeal mean anything, he should reach an elevated position in the game. He takes instruction well. Has a good temperament, and I'm having a lot of fun watching his progress."

But face-to-face he was deliberately reticent, for which I am grateful. It motivated me each and every day to accomplish something that might make him proud, just so that I could hear an "atta boy" from him. When he said more than that—"pretty good game," after a Little League baseball game, for instance—that was the pinnacle for me. But I learned never to expect much more than that from him. His style clearly would have been out of place in today's world, where every kid gets a trophy just for participating.

Thus, I was not exaggerating when in the wake of my U.S. Amateur victory I was asked what he might have said to me, and I responded, "Don't let it go to your head, son." Dad was determined that the humility for which he was known was passed on to his kids.

The only time I lamented anything about being the son of Bing Crosby was when we were required to participate in Dad's annual Christmas shows or the Minute Maid orange juice commercials. It horrified me. I had somewhat of a reputation as a jock, even as far back as fourth or fifth grade. There were only three network television stations and a local station or two in those days, so when Dad's Christmas show came on television it was generating the equivalent in those days of Super Bowl ratings. In 1973, for instance, *Bing Crosby's Sun Valley Christmas Show* on NBC was seen by nearly fifty million viewers. Much of the country was tuned in and there I was, wearing an unflattering outfit and singing. I attempted to portray indifference, though it did not help. Meanwhile, all I could think about was the verbal abuse I was going to receive from friends at school the day after it aired. When I arrived, a group of forty or more classmates would serenade me, singing, "I'm dreaming of a White Christmas," or go "buh-buh-buh-boo," for which Dad was renowned. We did eleven of those shows.

I heard a lot of orange juice jokes, too. Dad had been an early investor in fast-freezing technology and as a result wound up a stockholder in, and later the chairman of the board of Minute Maid, the first frozen orange juice. We filmed commercials for Minute Maid at our home. For a cocky young kid who fashioned himself an athlete and by extension one of the cool kids, I was an easy target for my friends and classmates. My parents saw it differently, however. "We think it is particularly important for our kids to feel they've at least partly earned their own way," my mother said, explaining why they involved us in the shows and commercials.

I said once that my name was a burden only in that people had an unfounded impression even before they had met me or knew me, that I must be a rich brat. I enjoyed disappointing them. Yes, I grew up at country clubs and had access to some of the finest golf courses in the world. For that I'm grateful. But had I ever allowed that to seep into my behavior and acted in a way that suggested arrogance, my mother and father would have set me straight.

"I just want them to be nice guys," my father said once. "I don't care how big they are or how important. I'd just like them to be the kind that other people would like to have around. And I want them to be thoughtful of other people. I hate rudeness, thoughtlessness, and arrogance."

Whether I've always lived up to that standard is for others to judge. But I have tried.

I CAN'T SAY WHAT HAPPENED WITH MY FATHER'S FIRST family. I believe he had more time to spend with us, as his career was less a priority later in life than it was when he was raising his first four sons. Dad was a devout Catholic, who donated the proceeds from his recording of "Silent Night," one of his two biggest-selling singles (the other was "White Christmas"), because he did not want to personally benefit from a recording of a religious song. Every Saturday evening, the car was leaving for Mass at Our Lady of Angels at six. If we showed up a minute late we'd be chasing the car down the driveway.

Growing up in Spokane, Washington, he attended Jesuit schools, with all that implies, including nuns with paddles. I doubt that my father, with his first family, was appreciably different than other good parents of his generation who used corporal punishment.

Corporal punishment wasn't the exception during the 1930s and 1940s. This was especially true if you were Catholic. Gary Crosby, the oldest of four sons from Dad's first marriage, described in his book *Going My Own Way* details on when his parents employed corporal punishment. In those days, it was fair game not only for parents, but for nuns, priests who taught classes, and even piano teachers (my own threatened me with a ruler when I had lapses in concentration) to use it. Many Catholic publications still promote corporal punishment as a useful tool in raising children.

I do not want to engage in a rebuttal of a book my half-brother Gary wrote thirty-five years ago. But Dad's image was somewhat tarnished by it for past and future generations. Those who read it might have made up their minds that Dad was a bad parent to have treated his son in some of the ways described in his book; that Gary was there, so it must have been true.

Gary's book was promoted aggressively as "Daddy Dearest," a play off the title of the book written by Joan Crawford's daughter Christina, *Mommy Dearest*. The book became a bestseller and later became a popular movie starring Faye Dunaway. The book and movie received so much attention that it made the idea of trashing your famous mother or father a successful business model.

During Gary's and my childhood, which ranged from the forties through the seventies, corporal punishment generally was routine. It might have meant a switch, a belt, or the back of a hand. The Catholic Church and other religions endorsed the practice.

"There have been times when I couldn't tell whether I was Captain Bligh in a Hawaiian sport shirt or the cream puff of the world, for Dixie used to tell me that I was too lax, that I wasn't strict enough, and that I forgot our boys transgressions too soon," Dad wrote in his book *Call Me Lucky*. "She used to reproach me with, 'you punish them; then ten minutes later you're taking them to a movie. That's bad. You should let the memory of their punishment linger so they'll remember it.' "

Dad was overly concerned that his kids would think they're better than other kids based on their family's fame. As a result, he wanted us to experience manual labor, at the ranches or other jobs. He expected us to show up on time and to take advantage of the educations that were provided to us. Basically, he wanted us to have as close to the same experiences he had had growing up. He delivered mail on cold mornings, one of the many jobs he had before becoming a law clerk and then an entertainer. He was never above it and wanted to ensure that we weren't, either.

Needless to say, Dad was unable to defend himself from Gary's charges, and Mom and our family felt that denouncing comics or critics that were misrepresenting Dad and slandering his image would only bring more publicity to both the book and the comics, that it was best to just let it die down.

I am certain, though, that my father loathed having to use corporal punishment, but, as did so many other parents who similarly used it at the time, simply wished to produce respectable adults.

My mother, at any rate, was the disciplinarian in my youth. When she punished me, it was explained to me why I was receiving punishment, after which I was hugged immediately. But she was not averse to punishment, even giving her express permission to my teachers in grammar and junior high to use corporal punishment on me should they feel it necessary. This became clear to me in the sixth grade when I called my teacher, Gary Lyons, by his first name and then later called him Mr. Gary after I had been warned. My private meeting with Mr. Lyons resulted in his beating a desk with his ruler. Meanwhile, he had sent a note to my mother explaining my misbehavior.

My mother wrote him a note in return. "Preparation H may be a great cure for hemorrhoids," she said, "but there's no cure for a smart ass." Preparation H had just hit the market that year.

Mom also more strongly expressed permission for him to use corporal punishment. To this day I still call him or refer to him as "Mr. Lyons, Sir."

My mom was even more extreme in her views. She wasn't just pro-choice; she has said on multiple occasions, kiddingly, of course, "Abortions should be retroactive to the age of 21."

WHEN YOU'RE THE CHILD OF A WORLD-RENOWNED CELEBrity, it is clearly a challenge to create your own identity. I felt it was motivating, as did my brother and sister. We all were determined to make names for ourselves even knowing whatever we might achieve would never equal what our father did. My motivation to become a good golfer initially was to be able to play with Dad and not cause him undue delay on the course. Then I strived to beat my brother at something, or anything. I began to focus on competitive golf, knowing that that would be admirable in my father's eyes. Finally, I wanted to become a successful tour professional.

Yet, even if I had succeeded in professional golf, it would never have compared to my dad's accomplishments and what he meant to the nation over a fifty-year period. It was immaterial.

I have early childhood memories of Dad, in his bathrobe, taking me to nursery school after I intentionally missed the bus. He loved doing it. He began putting us in his Christmas shows when I was five. It didn't matter to him that some of us weren't talented enough to warrant an appearance in prime time. He spent a lot of time with us collectively and one on one. For myself, it was professional sports, on television and attending games. For Harry, it was hunting; the two of them spent ten to fifteen weekends a year hunting duck on the Sacramento Delta. For Harry and me, it was golf every weekend during the school year and every day on our summer trips to Guadalajara to play golf everyday; here my father would have time with his immediate family for the better part of a month each summer without distractions. For Mary, he took her to the theater to see shows and played tennis with her. He separately took Harry and Mary on African safaris, where impalas and crocodiles fell prey to their marksmanship. The crocodile, incidentally, reportedly had killed more than four villagers and was more than twenty-feet in length. When Mary, thirteen at the time, brought down the croc, the villagers celebrated and likely slept better as a result.

Dad had started this bonding process with us at a very early age and our participation in these events was something we wanted and to which we looked forward.

In the summer of 1976, our second to last summer of Dad's concerts at the Palladium in London, my role had been strategically minimized because I sang in the key of B flat and had my microphone turned down, or even off, by the producers. So I sulked. I was stranded in London for the summer and was able to play golf only when Dad set it up for me, about three times a week. Dad likely spent hours each week arranging golf and likely owed many future favors as a result. So when he saw me sulking he asked me what was wrong. I explained that I barely had a role in the show, that I was spending the summer there and likely neglecting my game, and that I wasn't much into show business at any rate. "I don't want you to do anything that you don't want to do," he said, "but maybe we can get you a bigger part in the show if you're up for it."

I had no idea to where that conversation would lead, but I promised I would do my best. The following week, there I was, singing a duet with Rosemary Clooney. I'm not sure that the audience enjoyed my effort as much as it did Rosemary's, but Dad was happy. So was I.

MY FIRST WIFE, CATHY, AND I HAD FOUR KIDS, WHO FROM an early age participated in recreational activities together—

skiing, sporting events, golf, swimming, and surfing. When we moved to Park City, Utah, we put our boys on skis at the age of two. By the time they were four, each was skiing black diamond runs, and the girls, born after our move to Utah, were close behind.

One day, my oldest son Nathaniel Jr. and his Uncle Harry were skiing fresh powder on a black diamond run. Nathaniel Jr., four at the time, glided through the powder and made it to the bottom. Ten minutes later, Harry, who basically kept sinking in the powder, arrived. I instructed Nathaniel Jr. to call Harry that evening and leave a message: "Sorry about Jupiter Bowl, Uncle Harry. We will ski the groomers tomorrow."

These were memorable days for me. I was able to sing my kids to sleep every night. I'd lie down beside them and attempt to imitate my father, singing many of his hits, including "Daddy's Little Girl," "Galway Bay," "Irish Lullaby," and others. This was especially fun at Christmas. It was also a way of instilling in them an inherent awareness of their grandfather's songs even though the renditions might have been beneath the standard he set.

My own parenting included a divorce. I had the four children from my first marriage and two stepchildren from my second marriage. All are adults now.

After the divorce, I was fortunate that my eldest son, ten at the time, chose to spend the vast majority of his time with me. The time I had with my other children essentially was rationed, as it is with so many fathers—every other weekend for four days. Visitation rights are hard for fathers, as it was for me.

It requires to an extent going soft on crime; with such limited access, it is exceedingly difficult to discipline them without incurring outright rejection.

I did not adjust well to accepting a compromised fatherhood. Still my wife, Sheila, as well as my former wife, Cathy, have made it work. We have six well-adjusted children who all get along; however, our house is known as "party central" for many twenty-somethings across Palm Beach County.

My Dad's idea of a curfew was the message that "nothing good happens after ten p.m." I was a bit more lenient. I told my twenty-one-year-old daughter, Bridget, as she was preparing to go out one evening, that "nothing good happens to a young adult after five a.m."

Dad had his way, I had mine, and somehow it worked out for both of us.

Being a father is the greatest privilege a man can have, with corresponding rewards when the experience is smooth and nonconfrontational. Treat your children like they're adults, I've said, and the transition is easier for everyone involved.

# CHAPTER 13

# OUR TIME TOGETHER

When I was a toddler, my father hired an Irish nanny, Bridget Brennan, and he deliberately chose her because she was also an accomplished golfer. She had been the lady captain of the Nenagh Golf Club in Beechwood, Nenagh, County Tipperary, Ireland. My parents interviewed several candidates, each of them undoubtedly qualified, but when my father learned that Bridget was also a golfer, well, she was hired virtually on the spot.

I loved Bridget (and later named my daughter after her), and we had a great relationship. She introduced me to the game in the backyard of our home in Hillsborough, California. We had five acres and no swimming pool; Dad had had it filled in, giving us more room to kick a soccer ball or to hit golf balls on a scale sufficient for a young boy, though initially I hit only plastic balls. She taught me the stance, the grip, and other fundamentals. I was eleven when she died, and I was at her bedside for ten hours that night.

I was fortunate as well to have a godfather, Jackie Burke Jr., who was an accomplished professional with two major championships on his resume. When I was four, he made up a set of clubs to fit my size. Virtually every day, Dad and I ventured out to the backyard, me with my junior clubs, Dad with a wedge, as he was trying to cure the yips that had plagued him off and on for years. He'd put down six or seven balls and hit chips and pitches in our yard and invariably would shank at least one.

At dinner one night when I was five, Dad told my brother Harry and me that he had set us up for golf lessons with Burlingame Country Club's head professional, Maurice Ver Brugge. "One thing I won't have is you arguing with your instructor over what he's telling you to do," Dad said. "You need to understand that he knows more than you. So follow his instructions."

I did, and I never regretted having done so. Maurie Ver Brugge became my lifelong golf instructor, and he justified my father's faith in entrusting our golf tutelage to him. He was a man of incredible integrity. He spent forty-eight years at Burlingame, forty-six of them as the head pro.

Dad would not let us join him on the golf course until we were good enough at least to get the ball around the course. Harry, being three years older than I, received the privilege before I did, which was the only incentive I needed to work hard to improve. "Nothing came on a silver platter for Nathaniel," my mother told a reporter. "It was difficult for him, being three years younger than Harry. Perhaps because of that, Nathaniel developed such depth. There was a time, you know, when Nathaniel was chunky and, well, awkward. And I felt so sorry for him. Still, it was then he found he had to earn the right to play with his father. And earn it he did."

When I was ten, though I was not yet a good player, I was good enough that Dad began allowing me to join him on the golf course. The following year, the summer of 1973, I went from an eighteen handicap to a six. At that point, we were equals at golf, and the game became the cornerstone of our relationship.

DAD HAD MORE TIME TO SPEND WITH HIS KIDS FROM HIS second family; his career, though still important, had become less a priority for him over time. "He was the best father," Mom said in an interview. "I think our kids were wish fulfillment because Bing taught Harry to play golf and to hunt, and he taught Nathaniel to play golf. He took Mary Frances hunting in Africa."

My father coveted his privacy, though privacy was difficult for a man of his standing. He was frequently interrupted by a fan or well-wisher. A wannabe cowboy longing for the solitude cowboys enjoy, Dad invested in wide-open spaces that guaranteed him privacy: a 20,000-plus-acre ranch in Elko, Nevada; a lakefront home in Hayden Lake, Idaho; another 5,000-acre ranch near Burney Falls, California; and an ocean-view house in Las Cruces, Baja California, Mexico, approximately 100 miles north of Cabo San Lucas and 20 miles from La Paz.

The ranches in Elko and Burney Falls clearly were getaways for Dad to go fishing, hunting, and horseback riding. They were also parenting tools for both sets of his children to obtain a work ethic. We spent the majority of our summers at the Rising River Ranch at Burney Falls harvesting alfalfa hay, working cattle on horseback, cleaning stables, and retrieving eggs from beneath defensive hens with sharp beaks.

These were fourteen-plus-hour days that I experienced from ages eight to thirteen, and I clearly remember counting down the days until I could return to the Burlingame Country Club and what I deemed to be civilized life. I even looked forward to the start of school.

The ranch was Dad's hedge against his offspring growing up as Hollywood brats. The intention was that the work would be hard enough to allow us to appreciate the contrast with the rest of our lives, as well as instilling a work ethic that would serve us well throughout our lives. My Uncle Leonard Meyer, who had married my mother's wonderful sister Frances Ruth, managed the ranch for Dad. He had a great personality, but he would become unhinged when we made mistakes on a cattle-herding day.

To be sure, the Rising River Ranch was a beautiful place, and we did do some trout fishing together there, as well as an annual three-day trail ride on Mount Lassen with a group of as many as sixty friends and neighbors. Uncle Leonard was often the trail leader, and these are truly special memories.

DAD OFTEN SEQUESTERED US, ALLOWING US TO FOCUS only on one another, enhancing our time together. Decades earlier, Rod Rodriguez, son of former Mexico president Abelardo Rodriguez, showed Dad some property in a remote region on the southeastern coast of Baja California, Mexico, overlooking the Sea of Cortez, about 120 miles northeast of Cabo San Lucas and basically in the middle of nowhere. The sea was flush with marlin for sport fishing and dorado for eating. "If we need fish for dinner, I go out at five p.m.," he said. "Otherwise it's not fresh enough. And I never come back empty-handed." And the weather was excellent.

My father and Rodriguez became partners in what became Rancho Las Cruces, as well as Hotel Hacienda and Palmilla Resort in Cabo San Lucas. Dad recruited his friend George Coleman, Desi Arnaz, and others to invest in Rancho Las Cruces, which included eight single-family homes and an inn with thirty rooms. There were no phones or televisions. There was a long-wave radio, with which we could get one station, from Houston, and the Armed Forces Radio Network. So we listened to Houston Astros games together, hoping to get news about the Pirates.

We had no friends there, either. We had each other and that was it, and that's what made it so special. The Sea of Cortez was akin to a trout farm for marlin fishing, and Dad loved it. It was his getaway and place where he could have family to himself.

We spent about six weeks there in April and May for a decade or more. My parents took us out of school and my mother, a certified teacher as well as a nurse, would home school us for those weeks, more or less. Usually less. These weeks represent what I call my educational void; in lieu of sitting in her makeshift classroom, I spent much of my time fishing with Dad, George Coleman, and other available friends

There was no golf course, but we still managed to hit balls on a rudimentary driving range of dirt and rocks about 280 yards long, with an artificial turf hitting area and small stones painted white that were arranged in circles to replicate greens. Instead of flagsticks, barrels were used for targets, marked in fifty-yard intervals. Dad, Harry, and I hit balls in ninety-degree heat in April and May. Then we'd walk out, pick them up, and hit them again. Dad easily could have paid some kids to shag them for us, but it was among the ways he chose to spend time with us. Dad, incidentally, would even go hit balls by himself and shag them himself in pretty intense heat.

At night, my father and I would sit on the porch together, listening to baseball games when we could locate them on long-wave radio, virtually our only connection to the outside world. On one occasion, the long-wave radio delivered rather distressing news. Among our neighbors in Hillsborough, California, was the Hearst family—Randolph, his wife, Catherine, and daughter Patty—with whom we were friends. In February of 1974, Patty, a student at the University of California, was kidnapped from her Berkeley apartment. Two months later, Randolph and Catherine had come to Rancho Las Cruces for a respite.

"Each morning, I walked the three-mile round trip to the club, and played tennis while I was there," Dad wrote. "The whole Hearst family, minus the kidnapped Patty, of course, is [there] visiting Desi Arnaz. It's their first respite since the event, and they've been gradually recuperating in spite of reporters and an attendant FBI agent, who turns out to be a decent sort."

The Hearsts came to our house for dinner one evening. Dad began flipping around the dial on the long-wave radio, searching for the Pirates game, when he inadvertently came upon a news station. The news that came across was that Patty Hearst had been identified as a participant with the Symbionese Liberation Army in robbing a San Francisco branch of the Hibernia Bank and was no longer a victim, but had become a fugitive. When Dad quickly turned the dial, Catherine Hearst yelled for him to turn it back.

"That was the end of the Hearsts' vacation," Dad wrote in his diary of the trip. "I got onto the ship-to-shore phone and arranged their immediate transportation back to Hillsborough. Of course, the Hibernia Bank is owned by good friends of the family, an ironical twist which the news hounds have fortunately yet to uncover."

The year before, my parents had bought a second home in Mexico, this time in Guadalajara, because, my father said, "it has the very best climate in the world for a golfer." We would go there for a couple of months in the summer and play golf together every day—nirvana for a father and son who were mutually obsessed with the game. The house was pedestrian—three bedrooms, nothing fancy—but it overlooked the golf course at San Isidro Country Club.

There was something magical about the way Dad insulated us at different points of the year. When we were home in Hillsborough, we had our circle of friends with whom we hung out. But when we left town, we had his undivided attention. Dad made time for the three of us—Harry, Mary Frances, and me—individually. He took us, one at a time, to the Big Island of Hawaii. We stayed at the Mauna Kea Beach Hotel, which had its own golf course, a Robert Trent Jones Sr. design adjacent to the ocean. We shared a room and played golf together every day for a week. This was something he wanted to do. and I'm glad he did. It ranks high in the storehouse of memories we made together, and I cherish them to this day.

Golf was the principal bond I had with him, but other sports contributed, too. A vast amount of our one-on-one time involved sports events. There was no cable television in those days and each sport typically televised only a single game each week. Dad and I would sit in his office and watch the baseball game of the week with Curt Gowdy and Tony Kubek broadcasting. When the game was over, we made the short drive over to Burlingame Country Club to play a round of golf.

Our favorite baseball team was the Pittsburgh Pirates; Dad had owned 25 percent of the Pirates since 1945, which provided special advantages. He usually took me into the Pirates' clubhouse before the game and invariably we found the great right fielder Roberto Clemente on the training table. Dad would spend fifteen minutes talking to Clemente in Spanish, and Clemente loved it. So did I. Clemente was my hero growing up.

One of the saddest days of my childhood was January 1, 1973. I recall watching the Rose Bowl game that day when broadcaster Curt Gowdy announced that Clemente had died the previous day in a plane crash while on a humanitarian mission. I was stunned. It was an extremely traumatic event for me. My father was among those to contribute to the Roberto Clemente Memorial Album.

When I was nine, Dad arranged for me, in full uniform, to sit on the Pirates bench next to manager Danny Murtaugh, who could fill a pint glass with tobacco spit if his team lost a lead. He and Pirates coach Bill Virdon doubled as a day care center for me whenever the Pirates came to San Francisco.

When National League East pennants were at stake in both 1970 and 1971, I invoked my Catholicism and prayed with Murtaugh in the dugout. Murtaugh, in fact, was seen on national television during the National League Championship series in '71, his head down, working his rosary in an effort to protect the Pirates' one-run lead.

The Pirates won their division in 1971 and advanced to the National League Championship Series, coincidentally against the San Francisco Giants. Naturally, we attended the games at Candlestick Park, but because of the magnitude of the games, Dad thought it important to expand our exclusive fraternity of two to include the rest of the family. So he invited Mom, sister Mary Frances, and brother Harry.

It was a short-lived experiment, one game only, a 3–1 loss to the Giants. We sat in high-profile seats on the third-base side, and any chance that Dad's identity would not be exposed vanished when Mom brought out her needlepoint, a large tapestry. She then proceeded to ask the fans seated to her left if they wouldn't mind her putting part of her tapestry on their laps. They agreed. About then, Dad changed seats with me to put some distance between him and the tapestry.

Mom soon realized that asking those next to her to hold part of her handiwork was a mistake when they ordered Polish dogs with plenty of mustard and began eating them over her unfinished work. Dad was virtually silent on the ride home, despondent over the Pirates' loss as well as the public humiliation. Our expanded fraternity, meanwhile, regained its exclusivity, just the two of us.

The Pirates advanced to the World Series in 1971, and Dad took me to Pittsburgh for the games. There I was in game five, in uniform and on the bench, sitting between Murtaugh and Virdon for Nelson Briles' two-hit shutout of the Baltimore Orioles at Three Rivers.

I had been warned by the players to be careful because the dugout was precariously close to home plate. As fortune would have it, the Pirates' shortstop Jackie Hernandez was hit on the wrist by a pitch and the ball caromed straight for my face. If not for Gene Alley reaching in to intercept it barehanded, it would have caught me square in the nose. It only delayed the inevitable, as it were. About eighteen months later, Harry completed the task when we fought over a chair in our television room. I've had three sinus surgeries as a result, though my brother has ignored my pleas to finance the procedures.

The Series games were played at night, which meant our days were free, and my father, as was typical of him, sought ways to keep me entertained. One afternoon, the Pittsburgh Steelers were practicing at the University of Pittsburgh. The Steelers were owned by Art Rooney, who was a friend of my father's, so he arranged for us to go watch practice. I was in the habit of requesting autographed pictures of athletes in those days. I met quarterback Terry Bradshaw that day and asked him if he would respond to an autographed photo request. "Absolutely," he said. So I sent him a letter, and a few months later I received a signed five-by-seven photo with a note from Bradshaw, while my father received a note from Rooney.

"Bing, it's great that you have delivered me a new and prom- ising Pittsburgh Steeler fan," Rooney wrote. "But please tell young Nathaniel that you spell Steelers 'STEELERS' and not 'STEALERS.' There's a difference!"

When Dad and I attended a San Francisco Giants or a 49ers game at Candlestick Park, he was there to spend time with me. He never went anywhere simply to be seen. We had season tickets to the San Francisco 49ers football games, just the two of us. Dad would walk into the stadium wearing a topcoat, a scarf, his Sherlock Holmes hat, and sunglasses and no one would recognize him, for which he was grateful. I remember one game in particular, when I was nine or ten. A few minutes before it was to start, he said, "I've got to go do something. I'll be right back." He then asked the other season ticket holders around us if they wouldn't mind keeping an eye on me. "Yes, of course," they said. "We'll watch him." The next time I saw him, a few minutes later, he was on the field singing the Na- tional Anthem.

The happiest times of my childhood were spent on the golf course with him. He enjoyed playing a threesome with my brother Harry and me at Burlingame. We played golf nearly every day when we were home. My mother said that Dad lived vicariously through my golf; although he never was a golf champion beyond the club level, he loved watching my own development as a player.

I was thirteen the first time Dad took us to Turnberry, a British Open venue on the west coast of Scotland. The first night we arrived, I was so excited about the extended daylight hours in summers there that after I had eaten dinner with the family, I went out to practice my putting. When Dad came to my room to say goodnight at about 9:30, I was not there. He had the entire Turnberry staff and the police looking for me for about two hours. They finally found me putting in the twilight. Dad was not certain how to react to my civil disobedience for not informing anyone where I was going. So he opted for forgiveness, having concluded that he couldn't be angry at the son of a golf nut for working on his golf game.

When I was fourteen, Dad wrote a letter to Ben Hogan and updated him on Harry's and my golf games:

> I still have a lot of fun playing with the boys. Nathaniel, the 14 year old—he'll be 15 this month— is looking like he's going to be a good player. He's a 2 handicap now at Burlingame, and he works very hard at the game. Takes instruction very well, and I'm confident that he'll make it—in some way or another—and at least he'll have a very good golf game the rest of his life.
>
> Harry, of course, is about a 6, but he is busy with music and he trains a lot of Labrador dogs and he has so many other interests that he doesn't devote enough time to it, but when he does get to play a little, he's pretty good.
>
> So I enjoy playing with them. They give me a lot of shots too now, you can be sure.
>
> Had a great time in Europe the last two summers with the two boys. Played all the golf courses in Scotland, Ireland, and England, and it was a great experience for them.

*They played in some Pro-Ams, too, and Nathaniel got
to the 5th round of the 18 and under Boys Championship.*

He enjoyed watching me compete. When he accompanied me
to golf tournaments, he wore his Sherlock Holmes hat and an
overcoat and often watched me through his binoculars from
a couple of fairways away. Or as *Sports Illustrated* once described it, "flitting cartoon-fashion from tree to tree." He did
not want me to know he was there, worried that he would
make me nervous or cause me to be distracted should he be
recognized and crowds start following him. So he wandered
the course alone.

On one such occasion, when I was playing the Junior World
Championship at Torrey Pines Golf Course in San Diego in
1977, Dad actually snuck up to watch me up close on the fourteenth hole and caught me in the act of throwing my club at a
tiny tree that had been strategically placed on the right edge of
the fairway to torment me. A subtle lecture followed, which,
alas, a photographer caught on camera.

Dad went mostly unnoticed during the course of the tournament, but memorably had no such luck away from the course.
I had encountered a most attractive girl about my age. I considered it my good fortune that she was Bari Brandwynne, the
daughter of an old friend of Dad's, Nat Brandwynne, then the
musical director at Circus Maximus at Caesars Palace in Las
Vegas. Bari also was playing in the Junior World.

"Listen, Bing," Nat said, "I've got to go back to Las Vegas
and do some shows tomorrow. My wife is staying behind with

Bari. Why don't you guys all go out to dinner together." I couldn't believe my luck.

So we did. The next day I shot a respectable round of 75 on the difficult South Course at Torrey Pines, after which we all went to a Mexican restaurant in La Jolla. We were all having a good time, especially my father. We had never seen him have more than a single drink, yet on this night he had three margaritas by my count. Then suddenly the revelry was interrupted by a woman in her late sixties, who recognized him from three tables away and came racing toward us.

"Bing Crosby, Bing Crosby, I lost my virginity to you when I was sixteen years old!" she said a little too loudly.

Everyone in the restaurant immediately stopped what they were doing.

"I lost my virginity to you!" the woman said again, louder this time as Dad looked for a convenient place to hide.

"I lost my virginity to Johnny McGillicuddy listening to you singing 'Moonlight Becomes You,' " she said finally, permitting everyone in the restaurant to exhale.

Dad had been horrified that a lady from his past might have been calling him out in front of his teenaged son and his newfound friend.

Bari, who has been a teaching pro at the Los Angeles Country Club for about thirty years, became a lifelong friend and an amateur participant in the Bing Crosby Pro-Am. She lost her father a few months after Dad died, sealing our commonality and bringing everything full circle for me.

# CHAPTER 14

# THE WORLD MOURNS

My father was fifty-eight when I was born, and I was reasonably young when the notion of his mortality began to occur to me. Since I was aware that he was of advancing years and that he wouldn't be around forever, I sought ways to bank time and memories with him. He was an early riser, up at 6:30, and he would have coffee and read the newspaper before the rest of the household awoke and shattered his solitude. I was probably in the sixth or seventh grade when I decided I would get up earlier than necessary and come downstairs and sit with him in the library. I did that for a solid year, though I don't know to this day whether it annoyed him or not, my interfering with his morning ritual and then fighting him over who first gets the "Sporting Green," as the *San Francisco Chronicle* sports section was called.

I had always loved spending time with him anyway, dating to my pre-school days—or nursery school, as it was called then.

I confess to deliberately slow-playing my breakfast so I would miss the bus and Dad would have to drive me to school.

Dad became sick in December of 1973 and checked into a hospital on New Year's Eve. The Bing Crosby National Pro-Am was played the first week of January in 1974, and for the first time since he began the tournament he was unable to attend. Two weeks of tests revealed he had a tumor on his left lung, caused by a nocardia infection. It was serious and surgery was required.

My sister, Mary Frances, meanwhile, had been attending school in Mexico at the time, against my father's wishes. He even quit talking to her for a couple of months. Finally, he relented and phoned her. "I'm about to have an operation," he told her, "and I want to ask you a favor. I want you to come home."

"Of course I'll come home, Dad," Mary Frances told him.

"I'm sorry about the way I acted," Dad told her, "but that's just the way I am. I'm not going to change now. But I want you to know I really love you and *I need* you now."

In an interview many years later, Mary Frances said, "That was such an incredibly hard thing for him to do—apologizing like that, admitting his need."

Dad was explicitly aware of his mortality at that point. He was certain he was going to die right there in the hospital. Meanwhile, Bob Hope and Phil Harris had stood in for him and hosted the annual party at the Crosby, and someone had recorded it and brought it so Dad could watch it. It was pretty funny, but some of it was bawdy and graphic. For instance, Hope had his hand in his pocket at one point. "Get your hand out of your pocket," Harris said to him. "They called the search off last Wednesday."

The jokes got worse from there. Dad generally loved a good off-color joke as much as anyone, but he was a devout Catholic who at that moment was making peace with God in the fight for his survival. When he heard the show, he got his rosary out; he was seriously embarrassed and horrified and actually mad.

He underwent three-and-a-half hours of surgery in which nearly half his left lung was removed. He was in the intensive care unit for five days afterwards. He received cards, letters, and telegrams each day from concerned fans, more than 10,000 total. When he left the hospital, he had to hire extra staff to help him send thank-you notes, a process that took two months, but was true to his character.

It was his awareness that his years were numbered, if not yet his days, that was at the root of his not wanting Mary Frances to go to school in Mexico or for my mother to do theater out of town. He once asked his friend George Coleman to "tell them what I was like," "them" being Harry, Mary Frances, and me. It wasn't necessary, considering the amount of quality time we had with him, but his concern was genuine and touching.

In the spring of 1977, Dad had fallen about twenty feet into an orchestra pit in front of a live audience during a performance at the Ambassador Auditorium in Pasadena, California. The orchestra pit was being lowered as the performer was to exit stage right. Dad unfortunately took a few steps in the wrong direction, and everyone watched in horror. Among those who were part of the show were a young Bette Midler, Pearl Bailey, the Mills Brothers, and comedian Freddie Prinze.

Dad was rehabilitating at home and had to cancel lucrative concert tours in Japan and Australia. Dad's old instincts kicked in, and he started to count the money he did not make as a result of the cancellations. So the gardening budget was cut back on our five-acre estate that had large eucalyptus trees that shed leaves at a pace that made raking them a futile exercise. Yet Dad insisted we do it. I remember thinking how he led by example, but I knew from a previous experience with Mom that raking eucalyptus bark and leaves one day invites raking them again the following day should a slight breeze come up. Here was Dad at seventy-four, with shoulders full of bursitis, electing to show me that when we weren't making money we had to do certain things for ourselves. But after a week, he caught on to the fact that with eucalyptus trees, one can never get ahead.

In early May, with Mom and Mary Frances in Dallas appearing in a play, I took my father to dinner at a Chinese restaurant for his birthday. He had yet to resume playing golf, though I was playing regularly and enjoying success of which I was quite proud. "Nathaniel wants to play in the Boys Championship over there again," Dad wrote in a letter responding to a fan in England. "He's been Captain of his high school golf team, which has just won the championship and he was low medalist for the 12 matches, so he feels quite full of himself now!"

He did resume his golf in the summer, while planning a European trip scheduled to begin at the end of August in Oslo, Norway. "We'll just see how it goes," he told an *Associated Press* reporter during a round of golf we were playing at Torrey Pines in La Jolla, just up the coast from San Diego. "If I can play as much golf as I do, I should be able to stand up for three hours on the stage. I don't work very hard anyway. But I'd hate to have to do any dancing."

On August 23rd, Dad arrived in London en route to Norway. "Boy, I would like to do the whole tour but it looks a bit tough," he told reporters. "The back is so bad that I can't even play a round of golf. I have to walk around with a four-iron and a putter and I can only manage nine holes. I told the promoters two months ago I couldn't manage the complete tour planned for Britain. But the pain is a day-to-day thing, and I may still be able to make it." He performed in Norway, though, then returned to London, and in early September began filming a Christmas special, *Bing Crosby's Merrie Old Christmas*. It was there that he and David Bowie collaborated on the song "Peace on Earth/Little Drummer Boy" that eventually would become an enduring hit, despite Bowie's initial reluctance to participate. Bowie agreed to do so because his mother liked Dad, he said. This song has become a true Christmas classic and is one of the leading YouTube hits every Christmas.

This was the oddest of couples, as mismatched as Dad's socks might have been. "The doors opened and David walked in with his wife," Mary Frances said in an interview. "They were both wearing full-length mink coats, they have matching full makeup, and their hair was bright red. We were thinking, 'Oh my god.' "

I said in the same interview that it almost didn't happen. "I think the producers told [Bowie] to take the lipstick off and take the earring out. It was just incredible to see the contrast."

Then they began and the connection was immediate. "They sat at the piano and David was a little nervous," Mary Frances said. "Dad realized David was this amazing musician, and David realized Dad was an amazing musician. You could see them both collectively relax and then magic was made."

*Washington Post* writer Paul Farhi called it "one of the most successful duets in Christmas music history—and surely the weirdest."

Following the performance, Mary Frances and I had school commitments and flew home. Harry and Mom stayed on and participated in Dad's Palladium shows, *Bing Crosby and Friends*. On October 12th, Mom flew home while Harry remained in London to study music and drama. The following day, Dad flew to Spain for some rest and relaxation, including golf and hunting. The first day there, he shot 92 and he and partner Manuel Pinero, a Spanish professional, lost to Cesar de Zulueta and Valentin Barrios.

They played again the following day. Barrios, in an interview he gave in 2000, provided a detailed account of the day. It read in part:

> He played very well and I know he enjoyed it very much. He told us he was feeling much better after his fall in California a few months earlier, and better still for being out on this beautiful golf course . . . I remember he scored an 85, he and Manuel won by one stroke because of Bing's handicap, which was a thirteen, I believe. Bing collected his ten dollar prize before we headed back to the clubhouse . . . He was driven up the hill in a golf cart and

only had a short distance to walk on flat, level ground. I was walking right alongside of him, the last person to speak to him. . . .

It has been widely quoted that Bing's last words were "that was a great game of golf, fellas" or something to that effect. Well, he did say that in the golf cart heading up the hill, but afterwards, while walking towards the clubhouse entrance just seconds before his collapse, he spoke his true last words to me. He turned to me and said "Let's go have a Coca-Cola."

He had died of a heart attack.

A week earlier, I had had a premonition of sorts. I was on the eighth tee at Burlingame Country Club when I saw the pro Maurie Ver Brugge driving up in a golf cart alone. When I saw him, I thought, "He's going to tell me Dad died." Instead, he was catching me up on the score of a game of some sort.

The following week, I was in my English class on the second story of Burlingame High School when the principal came and pulled me out of class. He did not say anything initially, but I knew it was about Dad. He walked me to his office and then broke the news. By the time I went out to the school steps to wait for someone to pick me up, a group of reporters descended on the high school looking for me to get a comment. I hadn't even had time to process the news.

My mother was thinking clearly enough that she had called a brief press conference at our home, a better option than having reporters staking out our house. Fifty or more of them were there. "I can't think of any better way for a golfer who sings for a living to finish the round," she said. She said she had spoken via telephone with one of the men with whom Dad had played his final round. "He told me that Bing had a very good round," she said. "I'd like that to be said."

For some reason, probably to be alone with my thoughts, I went over to Burlingame that afternoon and played golf. Dad would have been okay with that. Bob Roos, a friend of my father's who lived in the neighborhood and helped him run his tournament, was driving by and saw me on the golf course. He stopped and came over to me. Roos was as frank as anyone I've ever known. "Sorry about your dad," he said. "He was a great friend and we all loved him. Let me know when you want to talk about the tournament." That was the first inkling I had that I was going to be involved with running the Bing Crosby National Pro-Am in some capacity.

Dad died decades before the World Wide Web, yet word of his death seemingly spread at Internet speed. Obituaries quickly appeared in newspapers around the world, many of them recalling him similarly to the way London's *Daily Telegraph* did: "If breadth of appeal is the measure, Bing Crosby can hardly escape the title of the most popular entertainer in this century."

The tributes that poured in were in line with what one would expect when an entertainment icon passes away. President Jimmy Carter said in a statement: "For all the roads he traveled in his memorable career, Bing Crosby remained a gentleman, proof that a great talent can be a good man despite the pressures of show business. He lived a life his fans around the world felt was typically American: successful yet modest, casual but elegant. He revolutionized popular music, sang the biggest hit of all time, yet was a man who would be at ease in any American home."

Jack Nicklaus called it a great shock. He wrote: "Only recently we discussed the possibility of having a father-son golf match between Bing and his son, Nathaniel, along with my boy, Jackie, and myself. Bing was a big booster of junior golf, a subject that was close to him. His annual Crosby Pro-Am raised millions of dollars for charity through the years, and I always look forward to playing in it. In fact, his is the only PGA Tour tournament I have never missed since turning professional in 1962. His friendship is one I will always cherish. Bing will be sadly missed by my wife Barbara and myself along with the million of admirers around the world."

Memorial services were held from Westminster Cathedral in London to St. Patrick's Cathedral in New York City. Bob Hope sent a message to the New York Archdiocese in which he said, "It's a whole new world for me without him. A little shabbier, I regret. If friends could have been made to order, I would have asked for one like Bing."

The funeral itself was a small affair at St. Paul's Catholic Church in Westwood, near where he once lived in Holmby Hills. It was scheduled for 6:00 a.m. in an effort to keep it secret and not have it turn into a paparazzi event. The idea was Mom's; she was always at her finest in times of stress. Among those attending were Dad's closes friends: Bob Hope, Phil Harris, Jackie Burke, Jimmy Demaret, George Coleman, and Virgil Sherrill. The boys from his first family—Gary, Lindsay, Phillip, and Dennis—were also in attendance.

When the service ended and we were leaving the church, we were bombarded with photographers' flashbulbs. Hundreds of reporters and press agents were there. "God bless them for having to get up in the middle of the night to do their jobs," Mom said.

# CHAPTER 15

# GROWING UP FAST

Shortly after my father died, my mother assigned me the task of succeeding my father as host of the Bing Crosby National Pro-Am. I got the job by default, or so it seemed, especially after my brief conversation with Bob Roos. Mom's abiding passion and desire was to continue her acting career—on stage or in film or television. It was a point of contention between my father and her throughout their marriage. Dad wanted her home to raise their kids. She was now a forty-three-year-old widow, genuinely saddened at the loss of her husband, but wanting to resume her career. So she took a role in the stage play *Same Time Next Year* that was going to tour for several months. Harry, meanwhile, was studying drama in London, and Mary Frances was in San Francisco with the American Conservatory Theater.

I was the only everyday golfer in the family. I knew the game, and I knew what went on behind the scenes. Tournament manager Dan Searle, meanwhile, had called my mother the week after Dad had died and began crying on the phone and saying there would never be another Crosby tournament.

"There will be a Crosby tournament," she said as emphatically as she could, "and Nathaniel will run it."

When she made her decision public, she said, "The family feels that the tournament should be continued because Bing was so proud of it. He thought golf was the finest game in the world, and he wanted others to enjoy it as much as he did. And it was always Bing's wish that Nathaniel would someday replace him as host of the tournament."

The responsibilities I inherited were manifold: Handling 168 amateur invitations; 25 professional exemptions; public relations duties; hosting the Clambake dinner party for 1,000 volunteers and the tournament players; serving as the master of ceremonies for the entertainment that included Bob Hope, Phil Harris, and Rosemary Clooney; and doing the telecast—where I joined CBS's Pat Summerall, Bob Rosburg, Ken Venturi, and others, with the legendary Frank Chirkinian producing—and demurely offered my limited input.

There were also weekly committee meetings in advance of the tournament, from September through to the week after the tournament. I became the first student at Burlingame High to attend class with an attache case. These meetings were held in Monterey, a two-hour drive from my Hillsborough home. My presence that first year let everyone know that I would be continuing the Crosby tradition. My mom, brother, and sister did not attend the tournament for several years after Dad's death.

In addition, as host, I was required to deliver the introduction to open the telecast each year. The first year I pulled it off much like my father did; I had written, rehearsed, and memorized exactly what I was going to say. I completed it in one take, to the amazement of Summerall and Venturi. (The following year I was expecting the same but forgot the preparation part. Chirkinian finally received a reasonable performance on my eighth or ninth take.)

The value of the tournament was in the amateur invitations and the future favors that could have been called in as a result. Dad had never utilized the tournament for that purpose and didn't need to. He had friends from different parts of the world to whom he gave great leeway in inviting their own friends or business associates.

Dad always recognized the value of the marquee and responded accordingly. If Jack Nicklaus wanted to bring friends Robert Hoag or Pandell Savic as his amateur partner, that was good by him. It was the same with Arnold Palmer, who would bring Mark McCormack, founder of the International Management Group. But Dad had a cutoff point, maybe the top ten or fifteen professionals, whom he'd grant the privilege of bringing their own amateur partners.

I was determined to operate as closely as possible to how Dad had run the tournament. On the amateur invitations, for instance, as my father did, I leaned on Carol Rissell, the public relations director at Pebble Beach, to remind me of Dad's long-standing invitees so I would not forget to invite them again.

The beauty was that neither Dad nor I had an agenda, and these invitations were and still are very powerful tools. It's still a fight to get on the list and "future favors" have been and still are an ongoing event since the Crosby became the AT&T, where a committee governs this sacred and influential list of names.

For me, being so young, the lesson was and still is, "Know who your friends are." Everyone and their brother were sending me cookies and pancakes trying to get on the list. An example of "getting an arm around my back" was an invitation to play on a special private course that was quickly followed by a "How do I get an invitation to the tournament?"

My first year doing the invitations, Tom Weiskopf made a personal request to have his friend Marvin Redburn invited. I honored his request, and when the tournament came around, he sought me out and said, "Nathaniel, I owe you a favor." I was floored that a golfer I greatly admired was thanking *me*.

Even Ben Hogan sent me personal letters, politely asking if I would consider inviting two of his Fort Worth friends, Bob Gibson (an oilman, not the St. Louis Cardinals pitcher) and Gary Laughlin. Of course, I honored his requests.

Then there were the pairings. I had help with them from Dad's friend Bob Roos, one of my favorites. Roos had a master degree in grumpiness. He looked much like the cartoon character Mr. Magoo, and Harvie Ward nicknamed him "old football face." He was an accomplished amateur golfer and had been the general chairman of the 1955 U.S. Open at the Olympic Club.

Roos and I spent about ten hours every week, from the first of November until the end of January, assembling the pairings for the professionals and amateurs who were likely to play. The entry deadline wasn't until the Sunday before the tournament, so much of it was speculation. Occasionally, I got complaints for pairing an unknown PGA Tour Q School graduate with a business magnate, as I did with American Express CEO Howard Clark once. At a party two days before the tournament, I heard him complain that "Nathaniel has paired me with a qualifier. Can you believe it?"

I also attempted to continue my father's practice of extending twenty-five sponsor exemptions, an inordinately high number on the PGA Tour. Dad had used many of these invitations on local club pros who were also strong players. My instructor Maurie Ver Brugge was a perennial benefactor and actually finished sixth one year. This became an issue for me when I finished college and was turning professional because some of those with whom I would be competing for membership on the PGA Tour were college competitors of mine and were interested in sponsor exemptions, and I couldn't fulfill them all.

The Clambake party also came with potential pitfalls. I was responsible for introducing the talent, and one year I introduced entertainer Phil Harris, a mainstay of the Crosby, before I introduced Bob Hope. I soon learned that Harris wanted to come on after Hope. Harris took it in stride, but not before letting me know that my position was more complicated than I had anticipated.

I realized that when my mother downgraded me to a co-hosting role starting in 1983. Mom had inherited Dad's image and likeness, and it was her right to assign me the hosting duties and her right to un-assign me. When I did not acquiesce to her last-minute request to offer an invitation to her doctor's son, I was un-assigned. For the final three years that the tournament was known as the Crosby Pro-Am, she took on the role of co-host and became heavily involved with the invitation list. I continued to do the pairings with Roos, but now I was asking Mom if I could get someone into the tournament.

There were many instances in which my father had had issues with the PGA Tour, often resulting in his threatening to end the tournament. He was pressured once to alter the format by doing away with the amateurs in an effort to get it to conform to the standard tour event—four days, pros only. "We will not change," he said. "We'll cancel the tournament before we'll change."

In 1964, the PGA asked for 75 percent of television proceeds from tournaments, including the Crosby. "They're just coming in and saying 'we're taking over,' " Dad's brother Larry Crosby, who ran the tournament, said. "Have you ever heard of anything like that? This is worse than the Capone mob moving in."

The Capone reference did not sit well with my father. "I read this morning's papers about the Professional Golfers playing for television money," Dad wrote in a letter to Larry, "and I think we should take a firm stand, but I wish you hadn't made the remark about the 'Capone mob moving in.' It will only irritate them, and can't do us a bit of good."

A few years later, in a letter to Charley Penna, he wrote, "Getting ready to have the tournament again pretty soon. The TPD [Tournament Players Division] becomes increasingly difficult. They would like to cut the amateurs out entirely if they could get away with it—but I fight them at every turn."

In 1967, the PGA was adamant that the new Spyglass Hill Golf Course built in Pebble Beach was not ready to host tour players. Dad argued otherwise and had support from Samuel Morse, the man who had developed Pebble Beach. This was another occasion over which Dad threatened to withdraw his sponsorship of the event. He prevailed and Spyglass Hill has been a part of the tournament ever since.

Deane Beman became the PGA Tour Commissioner in 1974. Beman was an accomplished golfer, twice a U.S. Amateur champion and a winner of seven PGA Tour events while earning his law degree from Maryland. He retired from competitive golf in his prime when outgoing commissioner Joe Dey handpicked him to be his successor. He was stern, but he also delivered on behalf of the tour and its members. He laid the groundwork by making tough decisions that have made the tour what it is today.

The tour, meanwhile, continued to ask for a larger percentage of the television revenues, though. In 1975, with Beman the new commissioner, a new three-year contract called for the tournament to pay the tour 40, 45, and 50 percent of the television revenues through 1977. "Originally, the PGA had asked for 70 percent for 1977, but we cordially replied that if that figure stuck, we would be saying aloha to the Crosby tournament," Dad said in an interview. "We have 800 people donating their time. We have a committee that works for nothing. And I work for nothing. We're not putting forth all this effort solely for golfers. We want them to leave a fair share for the charities we support."

This was the backdrop to my becoming host. Despite the wonderful assistance I received from Roos and others, organizing the event was not easy. Crosby weather returned to the tournament in my first year, after several years of drought, and we had a rain delay that threatened to cut it to three days. Beman thought it was an opportune time to push his idea of eliminating the amateurs playing on Sunday, and he sent the tour's tournament director, Jack Tuthill, and Clyde Mangrum to negotiate with me. And because Tuthill and Mangrum were extremely likable, I caved easily.

"Well, okay," I said sheepishly, referring to Beman's idea, not knowing any better. Later that night, I met with George Coleman and told him what had happened. He said to go back and tell them to play to the contract. So I did. "I've been advised otherwise," I said the next day. "We're having the amateurs play on Sunday."

It did not sit well with the tour hierarchy, and Beman was not finished. Several weeks later, I played with him in the Pro-Am of what then was called the Tournament Players Championship (now the Players Championship, which no longer has a Pro-Am). Beman was seemingly great with me. He spun me with PGA Tour stories because he knew I wanted to be a golf pro. Then he'd weave in his mission, that they really need ten or fifteen spots in the Crosby Pro-Am for CBS, or that we don't want the amateurs to play on Sunday. I stood my ground, thanks to Coleman. I like Beman, who was very kind to me, but he had a vision of where he wanted the tournament to go, and it was contrary to my father's mission. And it was Dad's own vision to put charity at the fore. It was his insistence that charitable donations match the tournament purse; that if the latter went up, the former had better do so, too. Dad was adamant as well that there would be no change in the tournament with regard to professionals and amateurs.

"The pro-am feature of the tournament has always been part of its character," Dad once wrote, "and I don't like to see its importance diminished. Our format has been eminently successful and to change it seems unwise to me."

I won on this issue, and even to this day, the top twenty pro-am teams after three rounds still play alongside the pros in the final round of the AT&T Pebble Beach National Pro-Am on Sundays, as Dad would have insisted they do.

I was host of the Crosby for eight years, four of them during my college years. As educations go, I got a good one at the University of Miami; but I got a great one, and a memorable one, running the Crosby.

Others can judge whether I succeeded, but I'll defer to my father's friend, the columnist Jim Murray, whom he greatly admired. "Two years ago, a search for a successor as host was launched," he wrote. "They never thought to look in Bing's locker. There they found a young man who learned the game at the knee of Bing Crosby himself. They were looking for Bing Crosby II and Bing had left him for them."

Even had I continued to host the tournament, with the advantages it would have given me in my business career, I would not have had any greater sense of accomplishment. As I often say to my friends when I tell them I used to run the tournament, "I have fallen from such great heights."

# CHAPTER 16

# WINNING FOR DAD

Dad's death was devastating, of course, but ultimately it served to reinforce my motivation. I wanted to win for him. Initially, I set out to win the U.S. Junior Amateur Championship for him in 1979. It is the most prestigious junior tournament in the country.

I played in a Junior Amateur qualifier at the Wellman Club in Johnsonville, South Carolina, one of twenty-eight players vying for two spots in the Junior Amateur field. I shot 66, a course record, and won by seven. The Junior Amateur itself was played at Moss Creek Golf Course in Hilton Head, South Carolina, and I continued to play well. I was the co-medalist with Rick Fehr, who later would win twice on the PGA Tour. My success in the qualifier and the medal portion of the Junior Amateur cast me as a favorite heading into match play.

I was so determined to win for my father that I performed mental exercises each day in my room. I visualized success, how

I was going to start, daydreaming about winning for Dad. Alas, I lost to a future PGA Tour player, Webb Heintzelman, three and two, in the second round.

Over the next two years, I played well, won college tournaments and the Santa Clara County Amateur, and reached the quarterfinals in the prestigious North and South Amateur and the Trans Mississippi Amateur. And in the run-up to the U.S. Amateur at the Olympic Club in 1981, I had made it to the semifinals in the Broadmoor Invitational in Colorado Springs. Yet because I hadn't been an All-American or a Walker Cup team member, I was a prohibitive underdog.

Once I qualified for the U.S. Amateur at the Olympic Club, I made the decision to practice and warm up next door at the San Francisco Golf Club, where my father had had a membership and I became a member at the age of fifteen. It allowed me to focus without distraction caused by some of the mayhem ensuing at the Olympic Club stemming from my participation.

Meanwhile, I took what I thought was my father's contestant medal from the U.S. Amateur in 1941 (in fact, as I learned later, he had played in the Amateur in 1940) and put it on a chain that I wore around my neck for luck. My mother, attired in Dad's old sport jacket and hat, was conspicuous in another way. She insisted on following from inside the ropes.

My best college friend, Bill Hadden, a terrific amateur golfer from Connecticut who played in a couple of U.S. Opens, was my houseguest that week, as was Robert Wrenn, a future PGA Tour winner. Each had been eliminated in the first round of match play, and when I showed up for dinner that night they looked bewildered that I was still competing and they weren't.

When I won three more matches, Hadden called me from Miami, but rather than congratulating me, he left me this message: "I can't believe you're playing in the Masters." In those days, the four semifinalists all received Masters invitations.

For the semifinal, I again warmed up at San Francisco Golf Club. No one noticed my absence from the Olympic Club range until the field had dwindled to four players and the tee times were at 1:00 and 1:10 p.m. The other three players were on the range before me. Finally, I pulled into the parking lot in a Chevy van ten minutes before my semifinal match with Willie Wood was to begin. I hit a few putts on the putting green, and I was ready to go.

I fell three down with nine holes to play against Wood, but came back and won the match with three great par saves from bunkers on sixteen, seventeen, and eighteen. On the seventeenth hole, I had a 100-foot shot from a bunker that required I clear a second bunker, and I hit it to within "gimme" range.

The next day, only one player, my opponent Brian Lindley, was hitting balls on the range at the Olympic Club in advance of the 8:00 a.m. start. He might have been thinking I'd been in an automobile accident and that he was going to win by default. But I had been warming up next door at the San Francisco Golf Club all week and did so again in advance of the final. It might have served as an accidental psych job, some pre-round gamesmanship, though I had not intended it to be.

Lindley took a four-up lead with ten holes to play before I began rallying and played my way back into the match. I was animated in doing so, pumping my fist and furiously rubbing Dad's medal. I'd like to take credit for being the first golfer to use the fist pump made famous years later by Tiger Woods. The cover of *Golf World* magazine is my witness.

On the sixteenth hole, I hit a good drive, then followed with a horrible shot, hitting the ball off the neck of the club—a crappy, awful slice that landed in the middle of some trees. As I'm approaching my ball, I get within earshot of Bob Rosburg, the on-course reporter for ABC. Rossie, as he was known, was a great man and broadcaster, a friend of my father's. But his signature call as an on-course reporter unwittingly came when he evaluated a predicament a golfer was in and often concluded that "he has no shot." Sure enough . . .

"He has no shot, he's got nothing," Rossie told the television audience. "He's not going to get this anywhere near the green."

I muttered to myself, loud enough for a nearby microphone to pick it up, "I'll show Rossie." I had an extremely difficult shot, I'll say that, requiring that I keep the ball low enough to avoid tree branches and high enough to carry a bunker by the green. I pulled it off and wound up winning the hole with a par.

Then, for the first time all week, the sun came out from behind a cloud. I don't like to admit a psychological issue, but in those days I had trouble when my shadow was over the ball at address. It is an issue that a hacker might have, but not someone trying to win the U.S. Amateur. Now I had to hit the most important tee shot of my life and I was staring at my shadow. Predictably, I hit a miserable shot, pulling and popping up the ball. It was certain to go out of bounds when—divine intervention?—a gust of wind suddenly came up and kept the ball in play, albeit in thick rough.

Serendipity might have been another explanation, except that on my next shot another odd event occurred. A blade of grass flew up and hit me in the eye and slashed it. I thought it might have been mud or sand from the divot I had taken. My eye immediately began tearing. William Campbell, the president of the USGA and the referee of our match, examined my eye to see if there was dirt in it. There I was, in full trauma, on national television, with the match on the line. I played the rest of the match with tears streaming from my eye. But possibly more help from on high arrived when my opponent buried his ball in the greenside bunker, allowing me to win the hole and tie the match.

We both parred the eighteenth hole, sending the match to sudden death. On the thirty-seventh hole of the match, the first hole at the Olympic Club, I hit what I thought was a good third shot to a green that tilts away from front to back. But the ball hit about six inches short and rather than release to the hole, it checked up in the fringe. I was facing a twenty-two-foot, slick, downhill putt.

All those years when I was practicing my putting on the Burlingame Country Club's green, I pretended to hole a putt to win the U.S. Amateur and other important tournaments. This time, the last thought I had before I hit that putt was pretending I was back on the practice green at Burlingame. The putt took a full fifteen seconds to reach the hole and appeared that it might miss. Instead, it caught the side of the hole and fell in. Divine intervention again? I'd like to think so. Either way, I had won the U.S. Amateur Championship.

I leaped into the arms of my friend and caddy Joby Ross and broke his nose in the process. Then I went looking for George

Coleman. On the eve of the final, while I was putting myself to sleep listening to the Willie Nelson album *Stardust*, the thought came to me that if I were to win the next day I would give the ball from the winning putt to George. I finally found George in the crowd of some 5,000 and handed it to him, one of my fondest memories of that day. George kept the ball encased in a square Plexiglas container and on his bathroom sink where he saw it everyday, a reminder of the great day we shared. He kept it there until he died in 1997.

Former President Gerald Ford, a friend of my father's, had been watching on television and phoned Bob Hope to talk about my victory. "It wasn't just his putting, Bob," the former president said. "That young man hit a lot of greens with his iron shots."

"I had to agree," Hope replied. "There hasn't been a Crosby with that much accuracy since Nathaniel's sister, Mary Frances, shot J.R. Ewing."

That night, my mother and I went to dinner at the Burlingame Country Club with George Coleman and his wife, Dawn, and William Campbell of the USGA. On Sunday nights at the club, a buffet is served, and as I was leaving the buffet line to return to my table, the whole room gave me a standing ovation, including Secretary of Defense Casper Weinberger and soon-to-be Secretary of State George Shultz, who were there dining together, as they often did on Sunday nights for many years. Of all the great moments I had, that one gave me the biggest chill. I will never forget it.

Coleman took me aside and explained to me the number of emotional victories he had experienced with his friend Ben Hogan. He said that he had never felt as emotional as he did with my winning the U.S. Amateur. It was quite an honor coming from Dad's best friend, then my own friend, despite a forty-five-year age difference.

I received a couple of honors at the end of the year. I was named Florida Amateur Athlete of the Year. But one that I cherished more was receiving the Northern California Athlete of the Year award. Yes, it was a regional award in a large state, so it might not sound so impressive, but consider this: San Francisco 49ers quarterback Joe Montana finished second and Oakland A's outfielder Rickey Henderson, second in American League Most Valuable Player voting, finished third. This was the season of *The Catch*, as it forever will be known, a Montana pass to Dwight Clark in the end zone in the final minute of the National Football Conference championship game to send the San Francisco 49ers to the Super Bowl. The vote had taken place before that game, so maybe some might have voted differently given a chance. Or not. Some of the votes likely came because I invited many of the reporters to play in the Crosby and many others were hopeful to receive invitations.

THE NEXT YEAR WAS ONE TO WHICH I LOOKED FORWARD with great anticipation. The U.S. Amateur champion extended invitations to play in the triple crown of major championships: the Masters, the United States Open, and the British Open, the three most prestigious tournaments in the world.

The destiny angle from the Amateur resurfaced, given the fact that the U.S. Open was scheduled to be played at the Pebble Beach Golf Links, the course with which my father and his tournament were so closely aligned.

It did not begin well for me, but it ended well. In the first round, I triple-bogeyed a hole early on and seemed headed for a big score, but I turned it around on the back nine and posted a score of 77. The next day, I played exceptionally well. I was paired with David Graham and Bill Rogers, the U.S. Open and British Open champions from the previous year, and I held the tee on fifteen of eighteen holes. I made a nine on the par-five fourteenth hole, but I still shot a 73 and made the cut. Herbert Warren Wind, the renowned writer for *The New Yorker*, was following our group, unbeknownst to me, and wrote about it in his book *Following Through*:

> I must confess I did not anticipate golf of the quality he showed us. His technique had improved considerably since last summer. The arc of his swing was wider, his tempo slower and more rhythmic, his technique through the ball more assured. Indeed there was little to choose between the shots he played and those of Rogers and Graham.

The only amateurs to make the cut were Corey Pavin and me. Pavin was an All-American at UCLA and a future U.S. Open champion, who, as all amateurs do including myself, desperately wanted to win the medal awarded to the low amateur.

Prior to the last round and my quest to win the amateur medal, I was warming up and Toney Penna, my old friend and instructor, was watching me, and I could sense he was nervous in anticipation of my round. So he began critiquing my swing and did so relentlessly, causing me to tense up.

I finally stopped him. "Toney, I'm just trying to warm up," I said.

He proceeded to storm away and let me finish warming up on my own.

In the final round, I blew a five-stroke advantage over Pavin with four holes to play and was nursing a one-stroke lead over Pavin and was in front of the eighteenth green in two shots. I chunked my third shot short of a bunker and was left having to execute a full Phil Mickelson flop shot over the bunker to save par and secure the medal. Meanwhile, I saw Pavin behind the green, his arms folded, watching to see whether I'd pull it off. I took my wedge and threw the ball virtually straight up in the air and it landed about five feet from the hole. I made the putt to finish low amateur by a shot.

I began celebrating with family and friends by the eighteenth green. Toney Penna, meanwhile, I was told, was standing alone by the scoreboard some 100 yards away, weeping like a baby.

Both the winner of the Open and the low amateur were honored at the awards ceremony on the eighteenth green. I received my medal first. Then Tom Watson, among my golf heroes, received the championship trophy. It was one of my more memorable moments in golf. I was sitting next to former president Gerald Ford and directly behind the dais. It was a Forrest Gump moment for me, as I turned up in photos, sitting next to the former president and behind Watson as he received the trophy from USGA President William Campbell.

My efforts in the three Masters and two British Opens in which I played over the next three years did not measure up to the 1982 U.S. Open at Pebble Beach, where my year had been made.

Many considered my U.S. Amateur victory a fluke. However, I was the first U.S. Amateur champion to win the low amateur medal in the U.S. Open the following year since Jack Nicklaus in 1960. I won the prestigious Porter Cup, beating renowned amateur Jay Sigel, a two-time U.S. Amateur champion; won the Mid-Atlantic Amateur; and shot 68 in the final round of the World Amateur Team Championship to lead the U.S. to victory. I was also just twenty years old.

I don't discount Dad's influence and how he motivated me posthumously. He bequeathed to me his passion for the game and inspired me; and, as my friend J. Michael Veron, an attorney, acclaimed author, and a terrific golfer, so eloquently expressed in *Sports Illustrated*, "I don't know what tune Bing was humming in Nathaniel's ear, but the beat must have been perfect."

Terry Jastrow, an award-winning television director and producer, was producing the Amateur for ABC that day. "Not many people paid attention to the Amateur," he said, "but it was a magical moment in golf. I've done sixty-two major championships and I remember more of that one. Bing Crosby's son winning in San Francisco, with his mom there? You're supposed to be impartial and try to present a balanced story, but this was magical storytelling. One shining moment. Never before, never again."

..................................................

# CHAPTER 17

# AFTERMATH

I had qualified to play the European Tour in 1985 and was in Madrid, Spain, when the public debacle with the Bing Crosby National Pro-Am took place. Mom had informed me that the AT&T Corporation wanted to come aboard as the sponsor and offered $500,000 to call the tournament the Bing Crosby AT&T. I had objected, stating that the title of the tournament shouldn't be compromised, that it should be called the Bing Crosby Pro-Am sponsored by AT&T. Mom replied, as any good parent might, that she would take it under advisement.

I had played the Asian Tour for five weeks, then came home for a week of practice before heading off to play the European Tour. I stayed with my mother in Hillsborough and on the way to the airport at the end of my week at home, she informed me that I was right about not compromising on the name, that she had sided with me on the issue. Given that Mom never really allowed me to coerce her on anything, that should have raised my suspicions. However, I was focused on the upcoming Madrid Open and my rookie season as a professional golfer.

In the first round of the Madrid Open at Puerto De Hierro Golf Club, I shot a solid 70 and was pleased with the score, but was somewhat perplexed when about fifty members of the press were waiting for me at the clubhouse. I thought it odd that I would be worthy of such attention for a score that was decent, but would not be leading the tournament.

The press was there to get my initial reaction to the news that day that Mom had removed the Crosby name from the tournament my father had started thirty-eight years earlier. The ensuing few days are still hard for me to reconcile. If you were to ask my mother, even to this day, she'd say it was because I caved, that she simply had been negotiating and that the Crosby name would have remained in the tournament title had the family showed a unified front.

It was, in my opinion, sacrilegious to consider removing the Crosby name from the tournament. The likelihood of that ever happening seemed at the time more remote than removing Arnold Palmer's name from the Arnold Palmer Invitational would be today. Corporate sponsorships were still relatively new in those days and only about half the PGA Tour events had them in tournament titles.

The Crosby board of directors through the years had carefully been stacked so that our family had a minority position. Once Mom pulled the Crosby name, I spoke with her and we concluded that we agreed to disagree and that I would refrain from making any statements. Mom then stated through a public relations representative that I had supported her decision.

A secondary concern for me after speaking with Mom's advisor was that she thought we could take our tournament and move it to Peacock Gap Golf Club in Marin County, twenty-five miles north of San Francisco. It was at that point that I put my foot in the door. I wanted to see whether it was possible to undo her decision to remove the Crosby name from the tournament.

The tournament was Dad's legacy. Eventually we were going to have to share the powerful and valuable amateur invitations, but Dad's name belonged in the tournament title in perpetuity, even alongside a corporate sponsor.

The board of directors essentially voted to allow the name change, though it invited my brother Harry and me to remain on the board. Harry and I discussed the situation and accepted the offer, still hoping to talk Mom out of her ultimatum and return Bing Crosby to the tournament title, notwithstanding our having lost control of the tournament.

Alas, there was no turning back once the board members exercised their authority and took control of the valuable amateur invitations.

Mom and I have reconciled our differences on this issue, but at the time it was a stressful issue for her, Harry, and myself. Mom was certain (and likely still is) that the board was going to buckle, given that the Crosby name was so meaningful to the event. Harry and I concluded that this was not going to happen.

Harry and I remained on the board of directors of the old Crosby for more than fifteen years before we were unceremoniously asked to step down, officially ending the Crosbys' association with the tournament. Harry and I played in the Pro-Am occasionally after that, most recently in 2008.

Because I had played in more than twenty-five Pebble Beach Pro-Ams, I told tournament office manager and long-time friend Cindy Zoller to tell the committee to remove my name from the invitation list for any future consideration. I explained that I had played in the tournament more than twenty-five times, and it was best to offer my spot to others who hadn't had that experience.

Or, as I like to jokingly say now, "I volunteered to be removed from the invitation list and then the bastards on the committee decided not to invite me anymore."

Mom, meanwhile, had endured some rough publicity in the wake of her decision, but she then received an offer from North Carolina Governor James Martin to come to North Carolina to start another Crosby tournament, featuring celebrities and amateurs.

Paul Fulton, the former head of the textile division of the Sara Lee Corporation and Bassett Furniture Industries, stepped up to spearhead the sponsor recruitment efforts.

Celebrities played a role in this Crosby tournament, too, though instead of professional golfers, they were paired with amateurs. This was no B list of celebrities, either; Michael Jordan, Bob Cousy, Bill Russell, Julius Erving, Johnny Unitas, and Joe Montana were among those participating.

The tournament ran from 1986 through 2001 and was quite succesful, raising more than $18,000,000 for state and local charities. Even Bob Hope, by then in his nineties, lent a hand, doing an hour show for 20,000 people at the stadium at Wake Forest University. "Bing would be so delighted to see what happened here, to think that something that started out as fun and remained fun has grown to do big-time good," Mom said in 1994.

The benevolence continues to this day through the Crosby Scholars, a program that began in 1992 and has leveraged $44 million in financial aid for students in the Winston-Salem, North Carolina, area. My mother still has a one-day event, a golf tournament called the Crosby Scholars Invitational that generates hundreds of thousands of dollars each year. This is where Mom really created her own legacy, an important one in its own right, benefitting thousands through the years.

My oldest son Nathaniel Jr., twenty-five, is a Tulane graduate who has a one handicap while he works the local Bear's Club membership for insurance business. My mother was on the phone with him, after which he came running out to the driveway to tell me some exciting news.

"Dad, you'll never guess what," he said. "Grandma said she'll pay my entry fee to play in the Crosby tournament. I just told her that this has to be the greatest day ever." Then I broke the news to him.

"Nathaniel, that's the Crosby in North Carolina." He was immediately crestfallen.

There was only one Bing Crosby National Pro-Am and there was only one founder, Dad.

I PLAYED THE EUROPEAN TOUR FOR THREE YEARS AND FIN-ished 87th, 115th, and 158th on its money list. As they say on

Wall Street, I was "negative trending." It was nonetheless a great experience playing a tour that included some of the finest players of that generation, including Seve Ballesteros, Bernhard Langer, Nick Faldo, Sandy Lyle, Greg Norman, and Ian Woosnam. The successes might have been few, but memories abound and involve incredible characters from all over the world.

One of them was a Brazilian bachelor, Jaime Gonzalez, a winner on the European Tour. I once spotted him buying a bottle of women's cologne in the Duty Free shop at Heathrow Airport in London.

"Jaime, who are you buying the perfume for?" I asked.

"You know, Nathaniel," he said, "I buy this bottle of perfume for a girl I have yet to meet."

I now use this line with my wife when she wins an argument. "You know, Sheila, I will one day leave you for a girl I have yet to meet."

Yet another great character was South African John Bland, a great player with little notoriety. He was a tough codger well into his forties and happy to attempt to intimidate younger professionals such as myself. We played many practice rounds together, and a typical exchange was his seeing me on the practice green and, a cigarette hanging from his mouth, saying to me in in his thick Boer accent, "Nat. So good to see you my boy. I'm telling you man, I thought about you yesterday and I bought you theater tickets for this weekend, because I know that you won't be making the cut."

Not too helpful with my fragile psyche.

One year, the great Irish player Des Smythe and I were playing what then was called the Spalding Tournament at Pebble
Beach when Des approached me and asked if I could host him
and his friend at the San Francisco Golf Club the following
week. His friend was Irish billionaire Ben Dunne. I obliged.
On the third tee, Des approached me out of earshot of Ben and
suggested that we play for a little money, that Ben loves to bet
and never wins. I agreed, but only if we kept it to a reasonable
sum, a $10 or $20 Nassau. No, Des said, he wants to play for a
thousand dollars a hole. I was twenty-four and could not afford
to wager that much.

"Listen, I guarantee your losses and you can keep your winnings," Des said. "It's that sure of a bet."

So I accepted and won $4,000 over the next three hours. In
the bar afterwards, they taught me how to play Spoof, a popular Irish dice game. It took less than an hour to lose the $4,000
plus an additional $500, and I had to sign for the golf and the
bar bill afterwards.

It was a costly lesson learned.

Another character was Irishman Christy O Conner Jr., a
great player who once finished second in the British. Christy
was a big fan of my former beloved, Cathy, the mother of my
children. I introduced her as my fiancée for the better part of
the three years when I played in Europe.

"Nathaniel," he said in his Irish brogue, "if you don't marry
that girl Cathy, I'm going to marry her myself."

Christy later promoted Orlimar equipment for us on the Senior PGA Tour, and Cathy and I divorced. I was having a few

drinks with Christy after golf a few years ago and was recalling how he encouraged me to marry her.

"Christy," I said, "would you mind helping me with some of my spousal allowance?"

Perhaps the most prophetic story came after the first round of the Jersey Open on the isle of Jersey in the Channel Islands. We were playing at the La Moye Golf Club, founded in 1902. The small clubhouse hadn't been modified or improved since then. After signing my scorecard, I had to alleviate a stomach issue that had been bothering me and repaired to a stall in the lean clubhouse facilities. Meanwhile, two British codgers who had followed me through much of the round, were there, too, at the urinals, but only one had seen me enter the stall.

"I do believe that young Crosby is going to be a fine player, but I must say that I don't think he's achieved his true potential yet," one of them said.

"I believe you're quite right," the other said, "but may I say that I don't believe he will achieve his true potential from where he is sitting right now."

So, at twenty-seven, notwithstanding my having broken a forty-year-old course record at the Bayonet Course at Fort Ord in PGA Tour qualifying, I announced my retirement from professional golf to an audience of my girlfriend and Labrador.

I petitioned the United States Golf Association to regain my amateur status, which is a three-year process. But as I tell the story when asked how long it took, I reply, "Just one afternoon. I hit a bucket of balls for some USGA guys, who said, 'You're no pro,' and they immediately gave me my amateur status back."

Winning a U.S. Amateur is no small feat. Virtually every player that was in their college years or had just graduated from college that won the U.S. Amateur went on to become a successful Tour player. I was I believe the second youngest player to win the tournament, and in no uncertain terms was aspiring to be a Tour professional. So although I believe that I defluked the U.S. Amateur win with other successes in amateur golf, I am still uncertain as to whether I am an underachiever or an overachiever. Either way, that trophy sure looks good on the front of my SUV.

Anyway, at the time I left professional golf, Orlimar Golf was a thirty-seven-year-old boutique equipment company in Northern California, its clubs popular on the PGA Tour, notably among California's tour pro contingent. At the end of 1996, the company was struggling and called me in to talk. They asked me to consider becoming president of Orlimar, offering me 10 percent sweat equity in the company. Its revenues were about $1 million.

We met at Diablo Country Club, where I explained how hard we had worked to grow the Nicklaus Company to modest numbers. I told them I had strongly recommended that the Nicklaus Company execute a direct response advertising campaign—infomercials—though it opted not to go that route. I told the Orlimar people they should consider the infomercial option.

A year later, in January 1998, I joined Orlimar, which followed through on my infomercial suggestion. Orlimar went from $1 million in sales in 1997 to $85 million in sales in 1998, the fastest growth year to year in the history of the golf equipment business. Moreover, our product became popular on both the PGA Tour and Senior PGA Tour.

Wall Street began to pay attention, and we prepared to take the company public. We settled on Merrill Lynch to circulate our offering. We were scheduled to raise $60 million at a company valued at $400 million and telling houses such as Goldman and Lehman that they were late. The initial public offering was scheduled for the first week of September, and our timing couldn't have been worse. The Russian ruble had collapsed a week earlier, reeling the stock market and resulting in the suspension of all IPOs for the foreseeable future.

I continued working toward growing the company to $200 million in revenues the following year, but without any real cash reserves, we ended up losing control of the company to a group led by our new board member Howard Lester, the founder and chairman of Williams-Sonoma and Pottery Barn. Four years later the company was bankrupt. No one made money, a virtual impossibility. Now I'm fine with the experience, except for the occasional twitching and nightmares.

There was always singing to fall back on. Or not. I'm often asked whether I can sing like my dad. I always reply with a stock answer, delivered in a baritone voice and imitating Dad as best I can.

"Some say I sing like my dad," I say, "some say better."

Anyone who has heard me late at night at karaoke parties might or might not pay me to perform.

So, for the last few years, I've been concentrating on high-end fractional products and marketing of real estate instead.

I had a consulting agreement with the St. Andrews Grand, formerly known as Hamilton Hall, the building that serves as the backdrop of the eighteenth green at the Old Course at St. Andrews.

Now I'm immersed in coordinating a product for the ultra-affluent that will offer them quality housing and private golf courses in desirable locations—Mexico, Hawaii, South Florida, Arizona, even ski resorts—a timeshare for millionaires and billionaires, if you will. It's called AppleTree Societies, named after the original private golf society in Yonkers, N.Y., that was called the Apple Tree Gang, which became the St. Andrews Golf Club of New York in 1886.

It is not easy developing a new concept and coordinating the involvement of more than twenty-five private clubs that have to alter their membership docoments. One developer, when hearing what I was attempting, said, "Nathaniel, you must really enjoy pain."

It's hard work that invites skepticism from others. I blame it on Dad. It must be in my DNA to want to start something of my own, rather than joining an existing endeavor that evolved from another's idea.

It has not been all business all the time. Golf has remained an enjoyable part of my life. My father had been a regular attendee at the Masters; and I was fortunate enough to have played in three of them, though each time I was asked to leave on Friday afternoon after missing the cut.

In 1984, I played a practice round and the Par Three Contest with Ben Crenshaw, my partner in the Bing Crosby National Pro-Am. He won the Masters that year. Karma.

I have returned to Augusta National frequently over the years. I've attended approximately twenty of the annual dinners for its amateur participants there and was its guest speaker in 2008.

In the late 1990s, I became an honorary invitee to the Masters, a privilege accorded past U.S. Amateur champions, among others. It allows me to play practice rounds at Augusta National during Masters week and to play in the Par Three Contest on Wednesday, the day before the tournament begins. Everyone has their story about first tee nerves at Augusta National, but my first tee story is decidedly different.

In 2004, Fred Ridley, chairman of the competition committee, not only assured me that it was okay to play practice rounds, but at the Amateur dinner on Monday night he encouraged me to play. So on Tuesday I elected to play alone as late as possible, 4:00 p.m., in an effort to avoid large crowds. I got to the tee box at number one, with my credential and an Augusta National caddy with my name across the back of his white coverall. I intended to take three quick practice swings and hit as quickly as possible, when an Augusta National official, assigned to monitor the first tee, stopped me.

"I don't think so," he said.

He saw a man in his mid-forties, twenty-five pounds overweight, with a carry bag, a golf cap that resembled a fishing cap, unflattering khaki pants, and golf shoes that looked more like tennis shoes. I did not resemble a competitor. He probably had concluded I was attempting to win a bet from an old college fraternity brother.

I explained my situation and that Fred Ridley had approved my playing.

"I don't think so," he said again, this time loud enough for Augusta patrons to hear. "I don't think so. You're not on my list, and you're not a competitor."

Now, suddenly, I became the center of attention for thousands of patrons, as well as a dozen or so security guards. After a ten-minute standstill that seemed like an eternity, the official began to doubt himself and got on his walkie-talkie to check out my story. An additonal ten minutes later, he said I was free to play. I promptly walked 300 yards down the middle of the fairway and dropped a ball. There was no way I was going to hit a ball in front of that audience that had come to expect an arrest.

I've often played in the Par Three Contest on a course that features small greens and miniscule tee boxes that place the crowds virtually on top of you. The first time I played it my hands were shaking, a new experience for me. The night before playing it in 2014, I was dining with my twenty-four-year-old son Nathaniel Jr., who brought out the needle. "Dad, what are you going to be most worried about on the first tee tomorrow?" he asked. "A shank, a scull, or a chunk?"

Dad, in fact, started with three birdies before the inevitable collapse.

Another year, I managed to catch the ball on the right jerk (also known as my swing) and hit an eight-iron to two feet from the hole at number six to win closest to the pin, earning me a Waterford Crystal vase. When Jack Nicklaus was at our house at the Bear's Club for a party two years ago, I told him how embarrassed I was for all the Masters' contestants and the entire tour that I could win a closest to the pin contest at the Par Three Contest.

In the Masters in 1984, I managed to eagle the thirteenth hole and received a pair of Steuben goblets that the Augusta National awarded to those making eagles. Often, I've realized there is no suitable hiding place for them after discovering my wife's friends or children's friends drinking Tito's vodka out of my cherished possessions.

On the occasions I've been invited to the Nicklaus household, his crystals displayed throughout the house have to number more than a thousand, a substantial percentage of them no doubt earned for various feats at Augusta National, dwarfing my own collection. It's not good for my self-esteem.

My other annual enjoyment at the Par Three Contest is harassing Condoleezza Rice, our former Secretary of State and an Augusta National member. I'm an admirer, and each year I beg her to run for president. Every time, she replies that she campaigned with George W. Bush, and a political campaign is not something she is interested in doing for herself.

"Come hang with me for a month," I said. "I'll teach you how to be an expert in shameless promotion."

When warming up for the Par Three Contest in 2015, I was on the range next to Fuzzy Zoeller, who had partnered both Harry and me in the Crosby. Fuzzy asked how I was doing.

"I'm working hard on my game," I said, "to play through this thirty-five-year slump."

# CHAPTER 18

## DAD'S LEGACY

Dad's legacy is an enviable one, but it also is a complicated one. The sheer breadth of content from music and film alone is staggering, yet on the legacy front it is one-dimensional. This and future generations are likely to identify Dad's name and music only through Christmas. Every holiday season, Dad's voice is ubiquitous on Sirius Radio and commercial radio stations, not only with his recording of "White Christmas," but with so many other Christmas standards that he recorded. Dad's Christmas duet with David Bowie, "Peace on Earth/Little Drummer Boy," from his last television show, has evolved into a Christmas classic and one of the leading views on YouTube each December. The holiday movie classic *White Christmas* still is played on Netflix and cable television stations. This is not a negative thing, of course, but basically that's where it ends.

Dad died in 1977, and since then there has never been a concerted effort to promote or market, or even to maintain, his incredible catalog of music and film. Elvis Presley, meanwhile, died two months earlier than my father, and though his music catalog was not nearly as extensive as Dad's, a serious effort was put in place to promote his music, image, and likeness in perpetuity. The same holds for Frank Sinatra, the Beatles, and even Michael Jackson. Efforts continue to introduce each of them to younger generations.

My concern is that history will misjudge or misrepresent the contributions of the Bing Crosby brand generally and Dad's music specifically without a proper airing in perpetuity. Here's a reminder of why I deem that important: He was responsible for the most popular recording in history ("White Christmas"); charted 396 records (Sinatra had 209, Elvis 149, and the Beatles 68); was the number-one-ranked box office attraction five years in a row and was in the top ten on fifteen occasions; and won an Academy Award for best actor and was nominated two other times. Not to be overlooked was his domination of radio and television. Dad's radio shows aired for thirty-one years and featured his singing, his talented show business friends, and, more than anything, his easygoing style and personality that resonated with the American public.

The latter point was the impetus behind his becoming one of the principal morale boosters during World War II, both to the troops on the front lines of the European theater and to those on the home front. He was not averse to putting himself in harm's way to bring moments of respite to those risking their lives on behalf of the country for months on end. Moreover, he

helped raise millions of dollars in war bonds through golf out-
ings and shows back in the States.

It was as personal a relationship with the country as any
entertainer likely has ever had, and his success allowed him to
semi-retire. He still remained in the forefront of the public via
his annual Christmas shows that garnered enormous ratings,
his frequent Minute Maid Orange Juice commercials, the Bing
Crosby National Pro-Am, and his frequent appearances on the
*American Sportsman* television shows.

Meanwhile, he continued to record albums and eventually
resumed doing live concerts in his latter years, selling out the
Uris Theater in New York and the Palladium in London as well
as other venues. He was even a hit on television after his death;
our final Christmas show aired two months later and included
the aforementioned duet with David Bowie.

All told, Dad spent fifty years at the fore of the entertainment business in an industry predisposed to short shelf lives.

Then there was Dad's profound influence on golf. His
tournament came along at a time when golf was struggling
to find an audience. Then Arnold Palmer began hitching his
pants and swelling the ranks of Arnie's Army, while Dad put
his tournament on television with Pebble Beach as a stunning
backdrop. And suddenly television networks began pursuing
long-term contracts with the PGA Tour, the United States Golf
Association, and Augusta National Golf Club. The net result
was growing purses on the PGA Tour and growing audiences
across the golf spectrum.

"He really put golf on the sporting map," *Los Angeles Times*
columnist Jim Murray wrote of my father. "Before him, it was

hardly America's pastime. It was a game most Americans thought was played by Warren G. Harding, John D. Rockefeller and the people who owned steel mills and railroads. When Bing invited the golf pros and a few of his movie cronies to play in an improvised tournament down in Rancho Santa Fe in 1937, no one knew it at the time but he had revolutionized the way the game would be played."

His tournament's greatest impact was on the charitable front. He introduced to golf the pro-am format that is an integral part of virtually every professional golf tournament today and a principal contributor to the funds donated to local charities each year.

Dad was the first celebrity to host a tournament. Those who followed included Bob Hope, Glen Campbell, Danny Thomas, Andy Williams, Jackie Gleason, Sammy Davis Jr., and Dinah Shore, among others. Each of them to varying degrees helped take golf mainstream.

Dad, Hope, and Dinah Shore are all members of the World Golf Hall of Fame. A fourth should join them: Danny Thomas. When he was dirt poor, he made a vow that should he become successful he would build a shrine to St. Jude, the patron saint of hopeless causes. When he became a star, he delivered on that vow, founding the world-renowned St. Jude Children's Research Hospital in Memphis, Tennessee. He began traveling the country, raising funds for the hospital, and in 1970, he agreed to become the host of the PGA Tour's Memphis Open Invitational in exchange for the hospital becoming the tournament's charity beneficiary. Today the tournament is called the

FedEx St. Jude Classic, and it continues to support the hospital financially.

Then corporate America began to replace the celebrities, whose tournament legacies began to fade as a result. Today, the tournament Dad founded is known as the AT&T Pebble Beach National Pro-Am. The Hope, as it was popularly called, is now the CareerBuilder Challenge, the Dinah is the ANA Inspiration, and the Danny Thomas Memphis Invitational is now the FedEx St. Jude Classic.

Each of these four celebrities spent incredible amounts of time and energy on their respective tournaments. They oversaw committees and invitation lists and made sure that the proceeds were benefitting their various causes, for instance, the Eisenhower Medical Center in Rancho Mirage, California, which is the Hope tournament's primary charity to this day.

But they are largely forgotten by the tournaments they founded. It's understandable that corporations spending millions sponsoring these tournaments want their brands represented in the tournament titles. But my thought is that retaining the founders' names as part of the tournament title would serve the dual purpose of paying homage to them, while providing a measure of stability. For instance, the tournament that began as the San Diego Open in 1952 is still played today—under its thirteenth different name. It's now known as the Farmers Insurance Open, which succeeded the Buick Invitational, which succeeded the Shearson Lehman Brothers Open. So it goes.

In the same vein, Arnold Palmer should remain in perpetuity part of the tournament title of the Arnold Palmer Invitational. Jack Nicklaus' name should be closely identified in perpetuity with his Memorial Tournament. The same should apply with Byron Nelson and the AT&T Byron Nelson and Ben Hogan with the Colonial National Invitation Tournament.

And, of course, restoring Bing Crosby to the tournament that started it all. Maybe this generation of Crosbys, or the next one, can help push the hands of fate.

The legacy I deem most important concerns how he fathered me. His devotion to me, though often centered around golf or other sports, was not because of them, but was the result of his determination to spend one-on-one time, as was the case with my brother and sister, too. It was a bonus, perhaps, that our time together involved a mutual love of golf, sporting events, fishing, and hunting.

His time constraints, even in semi-retirement, could have been an impediment to our time together, but they weren't, and the results were incredible experiences and the memories they created: a one-time trip to Pittsburgh to watch the Pirates in the World Series, or an African safari. For me, my fondest memories tend toward his making me a part of his daily routine, whether it was playing golf or watching games together, or even the simple act of sharing the sports page at breakfast.

Dad was adamant that we grew up with an understanding of what a full day's work was, hence our fourteen-hour summer days bailing alfalfa and working cattle on his ranch. He was determined that we not become Hollywood brats, and the time we spent together helped on that front. He never steered us toward a specific sport or hobby. We took to them on our own, but we did so with the added benefit of fulfilling our mutual yearning to spend time with him. Hopefully my own children will follow suit, with a similar appreciation for the one-on-one time that is the reward unto itself.

Dad also provided me the legacy of befriending his friends, generational friendships that I maintained with Ben Hogan, George Coleman, Harvie Ward, Toney Penna, and Jackie Burke. It was a gift like no other.

I pinch myself that I was good or lucky enough to win a U.S. Amateur, but I'm thankful that I had the foresight to give Coleman the ball from the winning putt and that he kept it on his sink in a Plexiglas container, a reminder of the great day we shared together.

In closing, I wish that Dad had been around to have seen me win the U.S. Amateur. But that said, I take solace and have faith in the fact that he had a better view than the gallery or any television audience. I'm guessing that he and a few patron saints were using some serious body English to get that final putt to drop.

# ACKNOWLEDGMENTS

Outside research for this book began, appropriately, only a few steps from Bing Crosby's childhood home in Spokane, Washington, at the library at Gonzaga University, his alma mater. The authors wish to thank Dave Kingma, archivist/special collections librarian at Gonzaga for his assistance with the Bing Crosby Collection.

Lisa Scott, Ben Hogan's great niece and chairman of the board of the Ben Hogan Foundation, kindly shared correspondence between Hogan and Crosby, for which we are grateful. Thanks, too, to the always helpful staff at the Ziffren Library in Los Angeles, the best sports library in the country.

Anthony Mattero, our agent at Foundry Media, took an immediate interest in this book and never wavered in his belief in it. Thanks for helping keep it on track.

And, last but not least, thank you to Carrie Thornton, the editorial director at Dey Street Books, for believing in this idea and demonstrating extraordinary patience with the authors. And to Matthew Daddona, our editor, for his patience as well and for his expertise in shepherding the project through to the end.

# ABOUT THE AUTHORS

**Nathaniel Crosby** won the United States Amateur Championship in 1981, is a former European Tour player, and was host of the Bing Crosby National Pro-Am for eight years. He played in three Masters, the United States Open, two British Opens, and on winning World Amateur and Walker Cup teams. He is the former president of Toney Penna Golf and grew two major golf manufacturing companies, Nicklaus Golf Equipment Company and Orlimar Golf, to substantial levels. He is currently the founder and president of AppleTree Management Group, the managing company of AppleTree Golf Society that is coordinating thirty private golf clubs into an ultra-affluent golf membership program. He lives in Jupiter, Florida, with his wife, Sheila, and their six children.

**John Strege** is the author of five books, including *When War Played Through*, which won the United States Golf Association's Herbert Warren Wind Book Award in 2005, and the best-selling *Tiger: A Biography of Tiger Woods*. He has covered golf for more than thirty years, and now writes for *Golf Digest*. He lives with his wife, Marlene, and daughter, Hannah, in San Diego, California.